Absolute Easiest, Metal Detecting Guidebook

Easy to Understand
Metal Detector
Guidebook

*How to use guide with Tips,
Tricks and Secrets!*

*Steve Cormier
Copyright, February 2019*

ISBN: 9781798018491

February 2019
Duxpond Books and Publications
Author, Steve Cormier

Easy to Understand,
Metal Detector
Guidebook
How to use guide with Tips, Tricks and Secrets!

Copyright 2019 and beyond,
All Right Reserved, Steve Cormier

All rights reserved. No part of this book may be reproduced or transmitted in any form by any means, electronic or mechanical, including photography, photocopy and recording, or by any information storage and retrieval systems, except as may be expressively permitted in writing from the publisher.

Disclaimer: Well we try to make the information in this book timely and accurate as possible, we make no claims, promises, or guarantees about accuracy, quality or value of your finds, and expressively disclaim liabilities for errors and omissions in the contents of this book.

Absolute Easiest, **Metal Detecting** Guidebook

Contents

Introduction 10

History 15

How deep will it detect? 23

Enhance Your Experience 30

Your First Metal Detector 37

Discrimination 54

Notch Discrimination 57

Phase Shift 60

Ground Balance 71

Target VID Numbers 77

Where to Buy? 46

Features you may want 81

Search Coils 86

Types of detectors; quality, economy 102

Warranty & Service 111

Motion & Non-Motion 115

Storage 118

Pin-pointers 121

Headphones 128

Supplies 131

Accessories 139

Detecting equipment 150

Bench Testing 159

Absolute Easiest, Metal Detecting Guidebook

Metal Detecting Test Bucket 163

Testing Garden 167

Field testing 169

Signals; False, Good, Hot Rocks 171

Tuning Manually & Auto-Tuning 176

Trashy Ground 180

How to Swing your Metal Detector 182

Crosstalk 186

Best Frequency for Hunting Type 187

Metal Detecting Places 191

Basic Rules for Permission to Hunt 196

Grid Searching 201

Proper Digging Techniques 204

Electrical Interference 209

Pin Pointing (with your detector) 212

Cleaning your finds 215

Types of metal and objects 222

Iron 225

Coin shooting 228

Meteorite Hunting 232

Heavy Metals 237

Code of Ethics 240

Why Read Your Owner's Manual? 244

Laws 245

Archeology Laws 248

Care & Maintenance 250

Cautions 252

Trouble Shooting Guide 253

Understanding the Lingo and Slang 255

Easy to Understand

Metal Detector

Guidebook

How to use guide with Tips, Tricks and Secrets!

You'll thank me later, how can that be? Well… this guidebook will save you more "Time" than any of the metal detecting books out there. Yes, you are correct. They seem the same, but they are not! I know that your time is valuable and swinging your metal detector is the only way you are going be digging the lavishly wild treasures that await you!

How can these simple, yet powerful pages transform you into a treasure magnet? The bigger question would be. What will I miss out on if I choose the wrong book? The value you can expect within these pages is far beyond average. This is from multitudes of photos, diagrams, charts, comparisons, stories, examples, definitions, useful tips, resources, techniques, equipment and accessories, before the hunt, during the hunt, and post hunt help. These are just samples of the many topics within these pages.

With this knowledge and a small amount of effort you will become the treasure hunting expert in a short time. You will have the right to show and brag to your fellow treasure seekers with pride, all the hidden secrets and valuable items you have found.

Make the decision to be rewarded, be the winner, and become the smart treasurer hunter.

Be the person that finds the "Big One!"

By **Steve Cormier**

Copyright, February 2019

Easy to Understand

Metal Detector
Guidebook
How to use guide with Tops, Tricks and Secrets!

What makes this book "Special?"

Don't mistake this for a quick read.

The overall number of pages exceeds expectation; it has a multitude of drawing and illustrations, and many, many photos. With an added bonus... it's up to date, written in 2019. How could you possibly go wrong with an up-to-date book? We are here to help you gain years of knowledge in the pages of this book. This is one of those books that you read and keep in your detector travel bag. It's one of those books that will never see a shelf, and will become tattered, worn and dirty from traveling with you to the treasure sites.

You Finding Treasure - This is our goal, these words will give you a jump start into a hobby of fun, sun and treasure hunting, and this knowledge is just waiting for you.

Uncovering The Mystery - How many times have you stepped over your pot of gold, missed a great adventure or walked by forgotten history?

This is a Wealth of Information - A few evenings of written knowledge to save you many hours of aggravation.

Absolute Easiest, Metal Detecting Guidebook

This book gives you a practical advantage over your fellow hunters.

Within these pages are **basic ideas on how, where and why,** all the while grabbing your interest from a more experienced and seasoned detectorist. Giving you many answers to questions that you may not have even thought of.

The purchasing of a great **guidebook is an investment** in your favorite hobby. We have written this book for the unskilled and new to metal detecting individual, in a personal and easily understand way. This book has many visual aids and photos to help with the concepts and strategies.

How can this book help you?

- Starts out very basic while answering your entire question.
- We give you ways to test, practice and learn before the hunt.
- We help you solve the mystery of how your detector works.
- There is a beginner, advanced resources and where to look.
- Before the hunt, during the hunt and post hunting knowledge.
- Terms and definitions, plus of the lingo and slang.
- Explore ways to find gold, coins, caches, meteorites, and lost treasures.
- Guide you in choosing accessories that you need.

Here is a few of the many features and benefits included.

Feature - It's a Guidebook *Benefit - Useful tips & info*
Feature - Drawings & Illustrations *Benefit - Easily Understood*
Feature - Beginner's Knowledge *Benefit - Quality treasure*
Feature - Photo's & Graphs *Benefit - Where to buy*
Feature - Supplies & Accessories *Benefit–Awareness*

Introduction

The public thinks Treasure Hunter when the term "Metal Detecting" is spoken. This is far from the truth; we are hobbyists and enjoy the outdoors, fresh air, exercise and spending time with our friends and family. Our hobby takes us to the local parks or maybe out in the countryside. We love digging up the historical objects and trinkets with absolutely no monetary value. Now and then we will run across the find of the day, or even the find of the month. These few unusual items will give us the opportunity to bring them into the monthly club meeting or show a friend what we have found.

There are professional that work solely in the field of treasure hunting that use metal detectors, they need and require results of finding objects of value. This is different from what we as hobbyists want and desire. Sure everyone wishes to get rich quick from finding that one big cache, this is like winning the lottery at your local gas station. Yes, it does happen but not very often.

We are realist within our hobby; we learn and educate ourselves through expanding our knowledge in related areas, which in turn will help our odds. Plus, we work hard learning how to research new areas, including methods of recovery and how to preserve our treasures.

The term "finds or targets" could be as simple as finding an old railroad spike from a narrow-gauge train in the mountains near an old gold mining district. Another way to think of target is using your metal detector to scours the hillside of a snow sledding area that is dry most of the year and finds a few coins. Why is a snow sledding hill important? After that first big snow, many people crowd into these small dense areas. As they bounce down the hill their pockets are emptied and the contents are lost in the snow until the first thaw. This gives the metal detectorist the opportunity to find those lost targets.

There are many levels of this hobby and everyone has one basic thing in common. They are new to this adventure when they first start. Everyone also starts with a metal detecting machine that is beyond their knowledge and most likely an inexpensive model. This detector could be a preowned model from a yard sale or maybe they picked it up from a pawnshop. What is great about this newbie process is that as they learn, they pass their knowledge and machine down to a beginner and the process starts all over.

If you are one of the people that require the best money can buy, I say go for it! Read the owner's manual and jump right in. Your odds are the same as the guy that picked up his first machine at the big box store. Until both of these new hobbyists get their boots on the ground, and dig a few shovels of dirt, they are both new learners.

I work full time at my regular job and I am lucky enough to get a lunch break in many areas of town. I keep my metal detector in my service vehicle and do park hunting on my lunch. Do I get rich picking up loose change under the swings at the park? No, but I have found many interesting things, one was an old USA Olympic token, why it was there? I have no clue. But this "find" was a keeper in my opinion.

Not all of your finds will be keepers, in fact I seem to have a knack for finding junk, but remember not all junk is trash.

After over 15 years in the ground it was fairly well preserved.

I have shown the above token to non-interested folks that only look for rings and jewelry, they thought of my personal treasure was junk. The hobby is what you make it, not what another MD (Metal Detector) hobbyists opinion is. I found this token in 2014 and it will always be in my "keepers" box.

Will your finds be in perfect shape when you pull them from the ground? No, in fact you will need to become skilled at preservation and cleaning. There are times when you will do more damage to your finds then you have intended. We are not going to be able to be perfect every time, but the number of digs we do will give you the experience that is needed to dig a good hole or probe properly to keep your finds in the best condition possible.

There are methods and techniques that will be addressed within these pages that I feel are important and other not so much. Remember this is only one person's opinion, you should read and research what other enthusiast do. Always read the owner's manual that came with your metal detector. If you purchased a used metal detector and there is not one available, you should be able to find one on-line. Knowing the details and features of your metal detector are far more important, then the excitement of going into the field the first time and trying out your metal detector with the lack of knowledge and how it works.

Within this book, we will go into deeper thoughts of how, where and what to keep track of and ways to remember your finds. It's easy to associate the bigger finds with a place and time. By knowing the places that are played out, can prove far more valuable, by choosing not to go. This will give you the opportunity to find new places to hunt.

Keeping a log is valuable and tracking what types of finds and what areas you found these finds will be touched on within this book. Including; some ideas and different ways to help track your journey using GPS, writing notes or even snapping a photo or two to jog the old gray matter. I personally use a cellphone App to help with locations and finds. This is your metal detecting hobby; make the best of what it and use the tools that are available to you.

You have just started this new adventure and within these pages we will get you off and digging. This book will start out very easy at first, and then working your way into the specialized area of your choice. If you want to relic hunt, coin shoot, hunt beaches for rings or find the hidden stagecoach robbery cache from many years ago, it all begins with this single book and a metal detector that is within your budget.

I have had a metal detector since the early 1980s, it was used and given to me by a relative, it squawked at anything that had metal in it. It was an old Fisher and I wish I had kept it, but it is long gone. I remember… I went to a park with that old, heavy and worn-out metal detector. What I found was a handful of quarters. Not a single penny, not even a nickel or a dime in the bunch. Every time I drive past that corner, I still think of that day, almost 40 years ago.

Let me help you discover!

History

In the mid-1870s gentleman named Gustave Trouve' developed new electrical equipment that was used in the medical industry to help locate metal objects within the human body. The idea was to help with the extraction of bullets and/or metal objects, from human patients. This was the very beginning of today's metal detectors.

The next turning point in the history of the metal detector came when Pres. James Garfield was shot, by a soon to be assassin.

When Pres. Garfield had been shot in the chest, and lay dying from that bullet, the surgeons worked frantically to help the president but this bullet had mysteriously moved within his body and disappeared.

Out of this necessity Alexander Graham Bell worked day and night trying to develop a method to find this bullet, the same bullet in which the surgeons could not find. Mr. Bell used Gustave Trouve' basic ideas, along with his telephone technology, including electromagnetic induction to solve the mystery of Pres. Garfield's lost bullet.

The basic idea behind metal detecting machine came from this lost metal bullet, he called this invention the "Induction Balance Machine" its sole purpose was to locate metal objects within the human body without having to do exploratory surgery.

The crude metal detector was unsuccessful in locating Pres. Garfield's fatal slug, not because the machine did not work. It was because of the bed in which he was lying on had metal coils that rendered the machine useless in finding the lead slug embedded in the presidents chest. President Garfield died a couple of months later from infection of the wound.

Time had passed almost 45 years, in 1925; Dr. Gerhard Fischer worked hard and brought the first commercially available portable metal detector to market. Within 6 years Dr. Fischer sold his first metal detector and proceeded to produce them in a large scale. By 1937 Dr. Fischer was awarded a patent for the first metal detector.

It was soon discovered that this new equipment had a value; it was used in finding buried military mines during World War II. It was a bulky machine mostly consisting of vacuum tube technology. This technology was state-of-the art for that time period, and one of its flaws was it required an enormous amount of battery power.

Although these units had many restrictions and limitations, a new and upcoming gentleman started redesigning the metal detectors, Charles Garrett. He was an electrical engineer by trade, but loved the adventure and hobby of metal detecting. In his early days of inventing, he developed a metal detecting device that used "Beat Frequency Oscillation or BFO." These first machines had problems, one of the big issues was called oscillator drift or frequency drift is another way of describing what the early issues of these machines.

A few of the reasons for frequency drift happen when parts started getting old and worn out, temperature change, battery voltage drop, plus many other issue with the first design of his newly designed electronic system. With great diligence, Mr. Garrett set out to cure these problems. This is where the Garrett Metal Detectors began to emerge. His determination in producing the perfect metal detector led to the removal of the oscillator drift, and the beginning of radically new search coils that are still used today.

By the 1950s White's Electronics founder Ken White Sr. released his Oremaster Gieger Counter, a revolutionary instrument that did not require the use of headphones as it detected uranium. White's Electronics continues to be innovative detector design, and offers modern-day treasure seekers new innovations, as well as giving higher performance and

Absolute Easiest, Metal Detecting Guidebook

other conveniences; they have what many would say, is the best metal detecting equipment in today's market. This is not an ad for either company, but we must remind ourselves that the leaders in this industry are innovators.

As time moved forward, metal detectors became smaller and lighter as integrated circuits replaced oversized vacuum tubes. This reduced the size of the core technology and also required less power, shrinking the requirements for battery power. As time goes on these innovations will keep getting better, just a few of the new ideas that are coming out are on-board memory, integrated circuit technology, multiple programming, GPS location and much more.

I can't wait to see what the future brings us.

What is a Metal Detector?

If you wanting to find the bigger valued treasures, then starting at the bottom and working our way up the knowledge ladder will give you a greater advantage than your fellow "Know it all!"

If you were to look up the term "Metal Detector" on the web you would get a generic statement such as;

Metal Detector; *A metal detector is an electronic instrument which detects the presence of metal nearby.*

Let's expand on these thoughts just a smidgen. This device, your Metal Detector produces a signal that "sees," below the surface of the ground. This ground can be one or more combinations of soil, water, plant life, rock, or any of the combination of these.

Your metal detector send a signal down into the ground and when it "sees" a metal object it reflects that signal back up to the metal detector. Then the metal detector takes that information (the signal) and in most cases gives you a noise, beep, or a tone to let you know it saw this signal and/or reflection, of the object below the surface.

The control box is the part of the system that produces a signal and sends the signal down a wire to the search coil. This search coil has two jobs, the first is to send the signal into the ground, the second is to pick up the signal from the object it "sees", and sends it back up to the control box.

Remember, it is looking for metal, so in theory if its dirt or water and everything is working correctly there should be no signal returned to the control box. As with anything there are always exceptions to the rule, but we're trying to keep this basic.

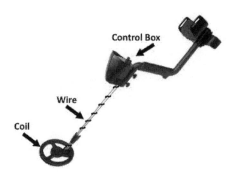

We have gotten to a point where we need a visual idea on the how the Metal Detector "sees" below the ground. The drawings below will give you a very limited and crude idea of how the signal is being processed.

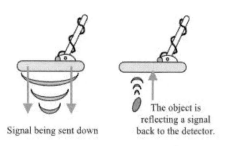

Signal being sent down   The object is reflecting a signal back to the detector.

We are going to be a little repetitive with the information we just gave you, and expand on it with more detail. If you are new to metal detecting this repetitiveness will help. But if you're an old pro it may be a bit redundant, so beware, it is done intentionally.

The basic idea is the MD (Metal Detector) pushes a signal down into the ground and when it sees an object, the object reflex a signal back to the coil. This then goes up the wire to the control box to produce a noise (audio or visual signal). Keep in mind we are still talking very basic operations on how in the simplest form a metal detector works.

Things can get real complicated real fast, if this is your first exposure to the hobby, then this will be a quick and simple way to think about how a metal detector works. I talk about objects and this term "objects" is generic, to a point. The metal detector sees "Metallic Objects." I spoke about how metal detector "sees," which is really incorrect. The metal detector sends and receives a signal that the control box understands.

Keep in mind this signal is affected by size, distance, type of metal, the number of objects near each other and many more conditions. We also need to remember that ground conditions matter, an example of this is; highly mineralized soil, it is more difficult for the signal to see the metallic object below. Why? The metal detector is getting many more signals, and it needs to "see" through this ground, but it cannot. Most metal detectors today are sophisticated enough to compensate for most ground conditions, including the multitude of items that can be seen by the metal detector.

There are a few limitations, and the biggest is "Depth," this is referring to how deep the metal detector can "see" (penetrate the ground.) When I referred to see, seen or seeing, I'm speaking about the reflective signal of the object.

With the more complexed machines, this signal is slightly different for the different kinds of metals. This allows the machine to decipher these slightly different. Once the metal detector processes the signals, it then gives us a different tone, visual ID and a way to "see or hear" before you dig. We will go much further on this topic later within this book.

So we are back to, what is a metal detector? With the little of knowledge from above we can easily say that a Metal Detector is a tool. A tool that looks on or below the surface of the ground and sees metallic objects.

This tool can be very basic or very sophisticated. They come in numerous brands, qualities, and sizes and can have features that are plug-n-play; while other features require you to study the owner's manual before being able to use them. I have been doing

MDing for years and still find many of the features hard to use or confusing without the owner's manual.

How deep will it detect?

How Deep?

This is the million-dollar question. Unfortunately, there is no correct or absolute answer. There are far too many variables which include the conductive properties, length of time the object has been buried, the capabilities of your metal detector, the size of the object, and even the shape of the object, as well as the search coil, circuitry design, and the environment. All of the above plus some is taken into consideration when we ask, how deep? Let's take a look at these different variables.

Conductive properties - The soil that you're detecting on has a conductive property, this can limit your detecting depth. The more minerals in the ground (mineralization of the soil) will make your metal detector work harder and will reduce the distance that it can detect below the surface. The soil mineralization varies greatly and can change within feet of where you're detecting. An example of that would be going from dry riverbed sand to nearby topsoil on the edge of the river bank. If you're fortunate enough to have a metal detector that has automatic ground balancing you can jump from the riverbed to the river bank easily, with very little adjustments to your machine.

That doesn't mean that you should not adjust your sensitivity or increase or decrease your adjustments on your machine; it means that your machine will adjust to smaller discrepancies.

Time your target is buried in the ground – Time can limit the depth your detector can penetrate. Because of this mineralized soil that we just spoke about can wreak havoc on metallic objects buried in the ground. This mineralized soil and water can create a corrosive action on metal.

We must think about and keep in mind that most metals corrode and deteriorate at different rates. Why is this important? Your metal detector doesn't see the object, it see the metal. A good example of this is the new modern zinc penny, have a very thin coating of copper on them which chemicals in the soil eat away at a very quick rate. Unlike the older solid copper pennies, silver dimes and quarters can take a much longer time to corrode or oxidize (rust). Gold is the exception to the rule, gold is not affected by corrosion in the same way many of the other metals are affected.

As these chemicals eat away at the metal, oxidation (rust) takes place, which is absorbed into the surrounding soil. This causes the soil to become more conductive, which in turn makes the metallic object appear larger and deeper than it actually is and easier to detect. This is known as the "halo effect."

Size of an object - The larger the metallic object, the easier and deeper it can be detected. An example of this would be an older car hubcap made of metal, compared to a silver coin. The larger object can be seen far deeper than the smaller object.

In cases where there are more coins in one hole, this is what we call a horde (also spelled hoard) which could be small or large. Your metal detector will see individual coins and not a horde as a whole. A more simplistic view of this is if there is a small leather sack filled with coins your metal detector most likely sees an individual coin and not the whole group. Because many times when a horde is found it is in a clay pot, a wicker basket, wooden box, or leather pouch.

From my experience I have found a coin spill. This is different from a horde, I spill is an accidental loss of many coins and a horde is the result of someone intentionally burying.

Here a short story of one of my finds.

I was hunting one calm and clear evening in the tall timbers of the Rocky Mountains near the Continual Divide. I ran across a campsite with the fire ring strewn erratically, as if the last person there was trying to find items they lost.

After prepping my detector and doing a few wide loops around the area, I started to become disillusioned from all the trash. I started talking to my dog, (she is a great detector buddy, she loves going where I want and never back-talks me.) Back to the story... the ground was thick with lead bullets, brass shell casing and aluminum trash.

I readjusted my machine to fit the conditions and tried around the campfire ring. Bang! First time I swung the machine I hit a good signal. This made me think I adjust the MD wrong, believe me when I say, wouldn't have been the first time I did that.

Feely funny about how good and fast I received the first signal I skipped over it. Then a few inches away I got another great signal. So I dug that one. There it was a coin, I pulled it from the ground double checked my hole and got another hit.

Nineteen coins later, I told my dog that I should be kicked in the pants for thinking I misadjusted my machine.

This example is about a spill of coins and not a horde. They were modern day coins and not one had any worth above their face value, although the lesson will last me a lifetime.

Shape of an object - The odd shapes of objects function much like an antenna, and consequently, their shape becomes important, causing you to detect deeper or the reverse.

Ring or loop-shaped objects lying flat, on or under the ground, produce the best results; shallow bowl or dish-shaped objects are similarly easy to detect.

Rod-shaped items, especially when scanned on end are very difficult to detect unless they're made of iron, which produces a halo effect, that we will talk more in-depth about in a later chapter.

The position of the object is important as well as the depth. Items that are long and narrow such as nails or wires can give false signal or lost signal, swinging your metal detector one direction but swinging the opposite direction shows up particularly easy.

Search Coil & Circuitry Design – Both circuitry and coil design can support greater depth, your limit your detectors capacity to penetrate. These items include the search coil size and design, including the overall quality of circuitry within your metal detector. Including what types of features and benefits the manufacturer installed into the hardware, and the software of your metal detector. You must understand that when the manufacturer designs this equipment, they tried to make it fit the largest number of users. When designing each model, they consider what types of metals are going to be searched for, including coins, relics, jewelry, buttons, bullets and everything from wire to gold nuggets. Their goal is trying to please the largest number of people with fewest models.

When they design a basic beginner model, many

features may not be included. When you compare them to the more advanced professional models, a beginner model may not have a large spectrum of features. This will limit you to finding objects at deeper depth.

Size of the coil also makes a huge difference in depth; the small 4 inch in diameter models may reach a maximum of 4 inches deep. The larger 8 inch models could almost double the depth to 8 inches.

The environment - This is a huge topic, there are many considerations and obstacles to overcome when considering the depth of how deep your metal detector can see. There are things such as the type of soil, moisture in the soil, electrical wires nearby, ground type, what is the weather condition such as thunderstorms, and outside interferences that may be nearby, such as another metal detector in near vicinity.

Some the other thoughts on how deep from an environmental factor would be, what kind target you're hunting, if you're in a trashy area, if there is large metal objects nearby or possibly fences, and, the orientation of the object in the ground.

Soils conductive properties - When your soil is heavily mineralized this will reduce the how far your metal detector can penetrate the soil. This mineralization can vary dramatically within feet. An example of this would be is if you went from a dry riverbed situation to topsoil. In most machines nowadays have automatic ground balancing. You can re-balance your machine manually to compensate for the change in soil conditions. In many cases, you would need to decrease sensitivity in other cases you would increase sensitivity depending on the conditions of the soil.

High mineralized soil such as areas that have black sand. There are things like hot rocks, coal cinders, saltwater and many other factors of our natural ground conditions that will either give you a little extra depth or do just the opposite and give you less depth.

How long the object is been buried - The kind metal that you're trying to detect can also affect how deep your detector can see below the surface. AN example of this is the new zinc pennies being made are very susceptible to corrosive conditions. Silver and copper are less susceptible, and gold will not have any noticeable to oxidation (rusting). Gold doesn't rust.

With the above information, the average basic metal detector with a stock search coil and reasonable conditions should be able to produce targets at these levels.

Small denomination coins *up to approximately a dime; between 4 to 8 inches.*

Denominations of a quarter, half-dollar *and similar size items; between 6 to 12 inches*

These depths are generalized, these depths depend on the quality of machine you have, and your experience and your ability to use the equipment.

Conclusion

Be on the skeptical side of any company that will tell you a metal detector would go deeper than 12 inches. Even these 12 inches is very deep because the average metal detector would do 8 to 9 inches in the best conditions. As conditions worsen so does the depth that a metal detector can penetrate. Just remember there are exceptions to every rule, and new ideas being discovered every day. Keep an open mind but be wary of false claims.

All metal detectors have a maximum depth and it is determined by the coil diameter, the physics of the search coil and the electronic circuitry of the machine itself. Having nothing to do with personal knowledge or experience in using the equipment. Plus the use of headphones with your metal detector will give you the ability to hear weaker signals that may be drowned out by ambient noise.

Enhance Your Experience

Owner's manual

Most new metal detectors still in the box will need to be assembled, most simple and easy. Do follow the instructions when putting it to together for the first time. Most first-timers skim right over the basics of how the machine is assembled and how their new MD works.

In reality, it is more important to understand how the machine operates and functions. Take a close look at your owner's manual after you assemble your machine read it more than once. Understand the basics of the controls and how to use these controls is very important. Once you get the basics down, take time to bench test your machine, play with the controls and if you're uncomfortable with any of its features, look for the telephone number of the manufacturer. Visit the maker's website and find a few YouTube video's helping you understand the features before you go out into the field.

The manufacturer is there to help you and a reputable company will take the time to answer your questions. Most manufacturers have a hotline or a service department to help you. They want you as a happy customer and will at least point you in the right direction to find helpful information, talk to you about their product, and even direct you to videos or information online.

This must to be said a third time... It is okay to read the manual more than once. I carry my owner's manual in my backpack when I'm out metal detecting. I do this for those times when I run into a situation that I just don't understand.

The owner's manual should be the first place you should go to troubleshoot any issues that may come up. When just starting out, the owner's manual is as valuable as the detector itself. I've even gone as far as using plastic laminate and made a small card on a few of the newest features that I have not used, giving me the ability to glance down for a quick review.

Research

One of the biggest secrets of successful treasure hunting is doing your research. This could be done from old books, old maps, Google searches, reading old magazines, newspaper articles, Google Maps, or an online information services. Another way is to talk with neighbors, friends, and/or joining a metal detecting club. But probably the biggest thing about research is, the more research you put in, the better results you'll get. We are giving you a short and condensed right now and will visit research in greater detail in a separate section later on within this book.

Practice

Probably the best tip that I can give you is to practice, yes... you will make mistakes, yes... you will dig up numerous items that have no worth, yes...

there'll be days when the adjustments on your machine is off. You will have days where everyone that you went detecting with finds treasures, and you do not.

This brings me to another short story.

One Saturday afternoon a friend and both of our wives decide go out detecting for their very first time. I was excited to get my wife out in the field after years of her saying. "No, honey, you go have fun!" I am sure to this day the ladies just wanted to show-up the old guys, but they never have admitted.

I proceeded to have a short class and I really felt funny, mostly because the ladies never stop talking between themselves. After this quick lesson and me setting up everyone's equipment, I thought I would follow behind and pick up anything they had missed.

This secondary sweep was in good humor and not meant to do any harm, I was there to help and teach. After a couple of hours I start getting antsy and wanted to show my years of hard work and skill.

I made the decision to veer off on my own to find the "big one." The day wore on in lonely silence, not a peep or even a squeak. I started checking my equipment. Wouldn't you know it... the teacher forgot to check his batteries. I know the machine turned on, I could see the backlit screen, but there was not enough power to get even the weakest signal!

The moral of the story, don't get cocky and practice, practice, practice and check your batteries. Oh... I have been reminded and reminded again. To this day they have never let me forget.

Practice is important and so is a routine of replacing old used batteries with fresh ones.

Every time that you go out and you make small mistakes or you dig up junk, it will make you better in the long run. The term "practice makes perfect" fits our hobby. The more you learn about your equipment, accessories, and methods. The better you will become at finding the treasures you're looking for and many items you never had a clue was buried below your feet.

Be sure to observe the sounds and signals that your metal detectors telling you, practice with coins, soda can tabs, pull rings, gold rings, nails, tin foil, old pop bottle tops and any other item you may encounter in the field. Try each item by air testing and then put the item in the ground. When testing, swing your metal detector as if you were in the field. See what the differences are and the levels of tones. Do all this in the convenience of your own backyard; we'll go more in depth on this type of testing in the test garden section.

Keep a positive mental attitude. Don't expect that

every time you dig an item out of the ground that it will be valuable. In my experience the first few hours of your new machine, you should dig every signal and try to make a mental note of how it was different, the way it was different, the depth of the signal and if you're anal-retentive like I am, keep notes on your phone or in a notebook. This is especially true when you start going to multiple sites. Having a notebook and tracking times, dates and what you found, can be handy. Things like weather conditions, the time of day, the soil conditions and any other notes you may have on equipment, can help in the future

Being careful

Most treasure hunters agree that compared to a lot of other hobbies, metal detecting is probably one of the safest activities around. Nevertheless, a smart metal detectorist knows the importance of observing the following cautions:

It's very dangerous *to hunt in areas where electric lines, gas/water pipelines, bombs or other unexploded objects may be buried.*

Trespassing on private property *without permission can cost you more than an embarrassment; you could lose time, money, and equipment.*

National and State Parks*, monuments, military sites, etc., are absolutely "off limits."*

Be Careful and Mindful *when digging, underground conditions are unknown.*

Education

Keep this thought in mind, keeping attuned to potential rewards of items other than gold, silver, coins, rings and all the obvious items of value.

There are items that have great value that people throw away, here is an example.

An example of this is a friend of mine found an old "Bubble Up" soda can; it was in mint condition and had been sitting under the floorboard of an old cabin for almost 60 years. He almost threw it away, until I told him the retail value of that soda-can could be from $7 to $19. That is a lot of coins to dig up for one find, and if I did not happen to know that these old cans had a value, his whole day of hunting for coins would boil down to about a $1.15 worth of clad coins.

The Bubble Up can is just one example, there are many of these same stories told by any metal detectorist that you meet, keep an open mind and dig.

When is a good time to hunt?

There is no right or wrong answer to the question, "when is a good time to hunt?" I used to keep my metal detector in the closet, and when I had a free moment on the weekend, would make a dedicated trip to one of my favorite spots.

But this is not the case anymore, I now keep my metal detector in my vehicle, cleaned, prepped, with fresh batteries. This is because there are many times where I'll be out and about with an extra hour to spare, wishing I didn't have to drive back and pull my metal detector out of the closet. Now if I run across a park or a schoolyard that looks promising and I have a few minutes, I can spend my time using my metal detector, and not wishing I had it with me.

You don't have to make a complete day out of your metal detecting hobby. You can spend as little as a few minutes searching an old playground, or a nearby park.

Your First Metal Detector

Choosing your first metal detector should not be taken lightly. If you're going to a big box store, you need to remember that the salesperson wants to make a dollar off the deal. Just because he thinks a metal detector is the perfect fit for you does not necessarily mean that it is a good fit.

The big box stores normally only carry one or maybe two different manufacturers, and within those manufacturers there may be several levels of qualities and/or features in brand they carry. What is important is to not buy the first MD that you see. The below list will give you a good ideas of the many manufacturing companies, to choose from. This is not a complete list but is a good starting point.

Alphabetical List of Metal Detecting Brands:

(Please note that over time this detailed information can change. This is not a complete list; it is intended to get you started and be aware of the many different companies that build metal detectors.)

Bounty Hunter   www.detecting.com
Bounty Hunter, 1120 Alza Dr., El Paso, TX 79907
(915) 633-8354   info@frsttx.com

Detector Pro   https://detectorpro.com
Detector Pro, 21 Colfax St., Raritan, NJ 08869
(908) 333-2942   info@detectorpro.com

Absolute Easiest, **Metal Detecting** Guidebook

Alphabetical List of Metal Detecting Brands:

(Please note that over time this detailed information can change. This is not a complete list; it is intended to get you started and be aware of the many different companies that build metal detectors.)

Garrett www.garrett.com
Garrett Electronics, Inc., 1881 W. State St. Garland, TX 75042
(972) 494-6151 sales@garrett.com

Fisher www.fisherlab.com
Fisher Labs, 1120 Alza Dr., El Paso, TX. 79907
(915) 225-0333 info@fisherlab.com

Marko www.noktadetectors.com
Nokta Makro Metal Detectors, Istanbul
+90 (216) 415 56 86 info@noktadetectors.com

Minlab www.minelab.com
Minelab Inc., 123 Ambassador Dr, #123 Naperville, IL 60540
(888) 949-6522 info@minelabamericas.com

Tesoro www.tesoro.com
Tesoro Electronics, 715 White Spar Rd., Prescott, AZ, 86303
(928) 771-2646 Info@Tesoro.com

Whites Electronics www.whiteselectronics.com
White's Electronics, 1011 Pleasant Valley Rd., Sweet Home, OR 97386
(541) 367-6121 sales@whiteselectronics.com

XP Deus www.xpmetaldetectorsamericas.com
XPLORER sarl 8 rue du développement F-31320 CASTANET TOLOSAN France
contact@xpmetaldetectors-media.com

It is highly recommended that you use specialties metal detecting stores and websites; these are known be a good fit for the novices. These stores normally have more than one brand of detector and each brand will have variety of models and accessories.

It may not be in your best interest to have a friend tell you which metal detector is best for your needs. If your friend owns a particular brand or model that he has been using for years, he may have a bias and tend to push you in what they are familiar with. The suggestion that he may make, might not be up to date or economically viable for you particular situation.

New metal detector manufactures must keep adding new features, ease-of-use items and accessories that your friend may or may not have considered. We're not saying that your friend is not going to give you the best advice; he may just not be up to date on what's available with the features of different manufacturers.

What about buying online? I do this all the time. But, my research and due diligence is particularly tedious. Make sure you know what you are buying, and double check every detail. Most sellers on-line are honest and want to be square traders, a few are not. They leave details out if it will portray the item in a poor light. I really prefer to have the touchy-feely approach. I want to take the machine out of the box at the store and get my hands-on it, push buttons, etc.

There are many features of today's metal detectors that are really handy, and each manufacturer has many of the same items and a few features that other manufacturers do not have. This also goes for different models of the same brand name. Most manufacturers have a low-end model and an exceedingly expensive model. Remember the more money spent, will most likely include more features.

As you look for a metal detector, be sure you create a list of things that you may want or think you could use. Use this list to determine or reduce the number of choices. Your decisions now can and will help your metal detecting experience.

Factors to Consider When Buying

How exactly do you choose a metal detector and how can you know you are choosing one that fits your exact needs and expectations? Before you go shopping, you should consider several important factors to help you select a metal detector that you will use and actually enjoy whenever you go metal detecting.

Skill Level

When you consider your skill level, are you a beginner that has never used a metal detector before? Do you have a small amount of knowledge, this may be from metal detecting with a friend or renting a used metal detector from your local treasure hunting shop? Do you consider yourself an novice, intermediate, or an expert?

If your skill level is towards the beginning stages of metal detecting, an entry-level metal detector that has few basic features and the price point is fairly reasonable, may me a sound choice. This could possibly be the perfect "starter" metal detector for your skill level.

Our recommendation is to purchase a detector that is slightly above your skill level. Why? It is simple; you should outgrow these simple machines your first trip. Most individuals learn to setup, adjust and control their unit very quickly. Why not have a few of the nicer options. These options will enhance you experience

How are you going to use the detector?

Many times people tend to want a certain style of a metal detector, but the type of terrain that's available to them within a reasonable driving distance does not fit the detector they want. Example of this would be buying a metal detector that is made specifically to hunt gold nuggets. When the reality is, you would need to drive or fly to the closest place to hunt for gold. Not thinking your backyard has an ocean with beaches to hunt, giving you a place to hunt coins, relics and jewelry.

Consider your surroundings and the style of metal detecting you wish to do. Possibly a good general use metal detector with a wide range of features would be a good option to start off with.

Another viable thought is the weight of the detector; there are awfully heavy metal detectors and models that are fairly light. For a small woman, you may consider a lighter metal detector versus one that can challenge a large man.

One last thought, if you haven't quite figured out how you're going to use your metal detector, don't worry a lot about it. If you end up enjoying the hobby and you're like everyone else within this hobby, this will not be the last metal detector you will purchase. As you become more experienced and find your area of metal detecting that you like, you will pick up the metal detector that fits that area of the hobby.

What Will You Be Searching For?

Gold, old coins, rings or maybe relics. All are worthy opponents. Most of the parks, playgrounds and big grassy areas of the football field will have most of the items just listed. Although finding gold rings, an old coin is our main objective you will find far more nickels, pennies and quarters.

It's always best to take a few minutes and think about what kind of items you would like to find, while you're out metal detecting. Are you more interested in finding jewelry, old coins, newer clad coins or even gold nuggets? Then think about the areas in which you may be metal detecting in, such as beaches, mountainous areas, deserts, or possibly underwater.

These choices could make a difference in the type of metal detector you would wish to purchase. An example of this would be using your detector underwater; you'll need a highly specialized metal detector that can be submerged underneath the water. Another example would be using your metal detector to find gold nuggets, and there are specialized units that have been set up for you to do exactly that. There are also units that will cover a wide range of items and do a great job on the average everyday coin hunting and relics style metal detecting. Plus, there are even a few metal detector companies that have great machines that crossover. In one example is a unit that will detect small nuggets of gold, plus this machine can be submersed up to 10 feet deep, and find your everyday clad coins, old relics and everything in between.

How Much You you're willing to spend?

Prices run anywhere from under $100 for a used bare-bones metal detector and can go well above $1000 advanced model. Only you can determine how much you want to spend on a metal detector for your first try at your hobby.

With today's online shopping, you can spend the same amount of money and get a nicer metal detector with more options. Keep in mind that your local treasure hunting shop will have almost as good of pricing as an online dealer, this is because the manufacturers are trying to help the small shops.

Your budget is going to dictate how much you can spend on a metal detector, but keep in mind that you should invest in the highest quality metal detector that you can afford, without overdoing it. Just be sure that you spend a little time doing your research. You do not get fooled by an Internet company trying to sell you a child's toy. Finding a good company, with a good reputation, that will stand behind their product is very valuable.

Where to Buy?

Shopping for a metal detector

With any new hobby, trying to locate a place to purchase metal detecting equipment can be a daunting task. There are many choices most people will go online and search for the best product. I do not recommend this method, if you have a local metal detecting store and/or prospecting store, they will have experts that have used the products.

Many stores will have rentals, used equipment, older models, and new in the box. You can ask them questions, have them show you how the models work, air test, and my favorite, pick it up and do the old touchy-feely of the detector.

This may seem simple but if you go to a large box store or shop online, you really don't get a feel for how your metal detector will fit your needs. Plus, the salespeople in a detector shop will have the expertise and the years of knowledge that you just cannot get in the big box stores or internet.

*** NEVER!!! ***
*** Never buy online when there is a professional Metal Detecting Shop in your area. ***
*** NEVER!!! ***

I suggest you do your research online read as much as you can, purchase a book or two and become familiar with the different features before you plunk down a large amount of money.

Buy from local Metal Detecting Stores!

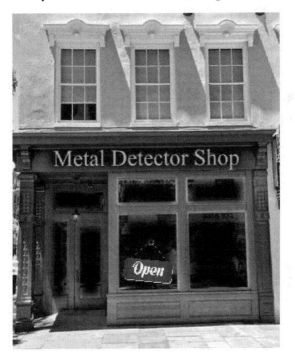

Support your local Metal Detector Shops

Educating Yourself

Remember, everything you purchase, you get what you pay for. Your purchase price should meet the needs you expect. The best example of this would be if you need a onetime purchase to find a lost ring in your backyard. You may consider renting a metal detector. Another choice could be the consideration of employing a metal detectorist. This can be done by contacting your local metal detector hobbyists, detector store and have the MDing club do this for you.

If you would just like to try the hobby out without spending a huge amount of money, then renting a metal detector might be the way to go. But remember, if you purchase an inexpensive metal detector your experience with the hobby will fit the price of that metal detector.

Purchasing local is always best, but there are times when this is just not possible and online is your only choice, the pricing is normally a bit cheaper than at a local store, but shipping can make the purchase higher than buying from an MDing store. You will be overwhelmed from the number of selection on the internet. If you're looking to find specific model, precise features and options within a price range, the internet may be a viable choice. With that being said, I still recommend buying, talking and using your local hobby store.

Stick within your budget and as you progress in your skills of metal detecting, so should the equipment that you use.

Each company has different makes and models. The price range is enormously wide, you can buy an inexpensive older used machine for under $100 or spend as much is $2500 for new and everything in between. Most of the time you could expect to find that each manufacturer has what they consider a low-end, medium-range, and a high-end metal detector. A good rule of thumb is to start with a midrange detector ($350 plus or minus) and after you have master your first machine step up to a nicer metal detector, $600-$800 range.

If you are a weekend warrior like I was or should I say bi-monthly warrior. A lesser expensive model was good for my first few years. But once I started detecting on a more regular basis, I enjoyed having the extra features that a higher end metal detector gave me. Plus, an advantage of using a lesser expensive model at first, is you can keep this metal detector after you purchased your nicer model and loan it out to a friend, so that you both can go hunting at the same time.

Shop Local

One of the worst things you can do to our hobby is to go into a metal detecting store speak with the owner or salesperson, learned all of their knowledge, and then purchase your metal detector through a nameless, faceless store online.

My theory has always been the store owners are no different from you and me. They will bend over backward to help you and in return, you purchasing from their store, no matter how small, make everyone feel better. This method will keep their knowledge alive and giving you a resource within your hobby.

Shopping online

There's always going to be a time and a place where your local hobby shop is too far to travel or they do not have the product in which you wish to purchase. Most have an online store and try to use their services first. I am finding more and more small shops going out of business because of the large online retailers. We are fortunate where I live that local metal detecting hobby shop is only an hour and a half drive away.

It's hard for me to say that purchasing online is okay, I truly believe in the small businessman. But there are times when free shipping, low prices, distance to travel, and the overall number of products available, makes driving a couple of hours unreasonable.

If you purchase online and your item is incorrect, broken, repackaged or represented as new and it's not, you were warned.

If your machine is coming from overseas, your detector may be a knock-off, not even be real.

There is a place for online stores, so if you choose to use one be sure it's a very large and very reputable online store. Check the return policies and the fine print before you spend a large sum of money. Remember the higher ticket items are, the far more likely there will be knockoffs.

Used metal detectors

Buying a used metal detector is a very quick and easy solution to spending lots of money on a brand new metal detector. Granted it may be a little older, possibly dirty and batteries probably need to be charged. It may have wear-and-tear or need to be assembled. Keep in mind this will give you a really economical way to determine if this hobby is for you. My first metal detector was purchased from a pawn shop more than 20 years ago. This detector taught me in an enormous amount about metal detectors, without having a large expenditure.

This may seem a bit obvious, but when buying a used metal detector you get the opportunity to pick it up turn it on and play with it for a short period before you purchase it. You can get a feel for how it acts and pick the brains of the person that you're purchasing from. It's an awfully good way to get a feel for all the knobs and buttons, adjustments and sounds that are common to that particular machine.

One of the drawbacks is you will not have the opportunity to pick the exact model you wish to use.

One of the positive things of getting a preowned detector is the price, these machines is normally economical. If you're just a beginner in this hobby and have no equipment at all, I would highly recommend this direction in purchasing your first metal detector.

Another place to look for used metal detectors is on Craig's list (you get to touchy feely before handing over the cash.) Although I have seen great deals, just beware that sometimes the previous owner may over value his machine. These preowned machines will give you all the advantages of purchasing at a pawnshop, plus you have the opportunity to negotiate the price.

Another great place to find used equipment is from your local MDing Club. Most members have more than one metal detector or know someone who does. A big advantage of buying from a club member is, they have the knowledge to train you.

Try to stay away from purchasing a used machine online, is not a good idea. There are far too many variables and most of the time the individual selling online will give you all the good points and never say one word about the bad points or issues. Buying a used metal detector on an auction site is not recommended, for the same reasons.

Renting Metal Detector

Many rental stores (Garden Shop, Tools Rentals, and Small Machine Rental Stores) will carry metal detectors that can be rented for the day or the week.

They are normally not a very high-quality machine and have been used by a lot of people that have no interest in our hobby. They are used, abused and are great for a short period of trying to learn a little about the hobby. But be careful if the person before you broke something and did not tell rental store it was broken, you will be responsible because you were the last person to touch that machine.

If you are in a desperate need to find a lost ring in your backyard, then renting may be an option for you. There is a difference between purchasing a used machine from an individual within the hobby and having multiple people using a rental machine for a couple of hours without any knowledge or interest in metal detecting.

Rented metal detectors have their place, just be careful if you try this method.

About the only exception would be is if you rented a metal detector from a metal detecting store (Treasure Hunting Store, Metal Detector Store or Prospecting Store). They will give you first-hand instructions on how to use the machine and make sure that you are comfortable with the controls and the features before you leave their store. Most of the stores have a variety of machines to rent, so if there's a particular model you have an interest in, they may be able to accommodate you in your rental choice.

Detector Fundamentals

Discrimination

If we were to define the word discrimination or look it up in the dictionary, it would read;

Discrimination: *Within the field of electronics, discrimination is the selection of a particular frequency, aptitude, phase, etc. affected by the elimination of another signal by the means of a discriminator.*

Sometimes it is better to have an experienced detectorist give you a definition instead of the dictionary.

A "Metal Detectorist" version: *Discrimination is a manual or automatic method of **unselecting** one or more types of metal and/or mineralization from the audio and/or visual signal, to make a metal detectorist hobby more enjoyable, by NOT digging every signal.*

Discrimination Principle

Metal detector discrimination is an important feature. This feature is typically referred to as the capability to distinguish between two or more metal objects. Discrimination gives the metal detector the ability to create an audio signal for the metals you would like to find and reject (silence) the metals you don't have any interest in and prefer to leave in the ground.

The drawback can be, but not limited to, missing an object because the items are in close proximity to another item of value.

There are different degrees of quality when we talk about discrimination, and it usually boils down to the quality of a metal detector you have. If your machine is at the lower end of the standard (this normally is quantified by price) the circuitry may not be as advanced. The discrimination portion of your metal detector doesn't seem very important, until you have dug more than your fair share of unwanted nails, foil, and other trash. Only after many hours of hard labor will your discrimination become important. Once the newness wears off of your machine, you will then stop and learn how to adjust your metal detectors discrimination and other features of your machine.

Variable Discrimination

Metal detectors that solely rely on audio tones to give you a clue can be basic or exceptionally sophisticated. There is no one single rule to judge the quality of a detector by the audio output. Many cases using an audio-only style of a metal detector is ideal. One example of this would be prospecting for gold with electronic technology or in layman's terms using a metal detector to find gold nuggets.

Fisher Labs has one of the better gold nugget detectors. There basic premises is for your hearing to give you the clues if your near a gold nugget or not. I have spoken to hobbyist that swear by this method and just the opposite from other detectorist.

Fisher Gold Bug-2 Metal Detector

The discrimination on many styles metal detectors have a simple method of adjusting the discrimination which could be as simple as turning a knob or pushing a button to gain or lose discrimination. Ther are two simpler styles of discrimination, the analog that uses a meter and digital uses a graph. The farther to the right you turn the knob the more discrimination your detector will have and the fewer types of metal it will detect. Which means you will not hear or see the items you remove from the list.

The picture below shows two types of discrimination which is used on the extremely inexpensive models. There has been a move towards digital displays with more information on the screen. Both of these models have a simpler style of discrimination.

Analog (Dial type) Discrimination

Digital (Dial type) Discrimination

Notch Discrimination

Notch filtering, also called Notched Discrimination is the ability of a metal detector to select which of the conductivity segments in the discrimination scale are active or disabled. If a segment is notched out, then metals within that level of conductivity will be masked and will not produce a response.

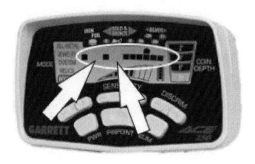

The white arrows show the nocthed out segments

In the picture above (white arrows) is a line of black squares with segments missing. The missing portion is the parts that have been notched out (Notch Discrimination or Notch Filtering). This is an adjustable feature in most modern metal detectors. There are different levels of this feature, including ways to customize and store your setting on many midrange and better detectors.

Notch discrimination can allow a window of desired targets to be accepted or rejected. You can notch out a particular range or reject everything except for the item you notched in or out. The notch could be widened or narrowed to your particular needs, within the capabilities of better quality metal detectors.

Below is another visual idea on how notch discrimination works. In this case we kept the penny and the ring setting, but eliminated the nails.

This notch filtered out the steel and iron nails.

If you have a notch filter, you can set your "notch" so nickels are still found even when pull-tabs are eliminated. That's nice, because a lot of places are full of nickels that other treasure hunters missed because they screen out pull-tabs and thereby lost the nickels.

Many of us think, "Who cares... it's only a nickel"
But what if that nickel is a 1918/7-D PCGS AU58
Key Buffalo Nickel worth $41,000

Phase Shift

Metal detecting discrimination principles are based on Phase Shift (also called; Phase Lag, Time Shift and Time Delay.) Since "Phase Shift" is how discrimination works we will discuss these principles in greater detail.

To get an idea on how phase shift works, look at the drawing below. The curved dash line represents the transmitted signal and the thin curved solid line represents the receiving signal. The small vertical dotted line and where the two curved lines meet, represents no phase shift within the two signals.

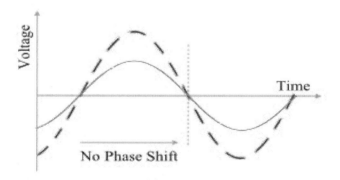

This is a graphical representation of "NO" Phase Shift.

Looking at the picture you get an overall idea of what the signal looks like, without any kind of metal object or coin within the detectors signal field. There are several things going on all at the same moment, we have power (labeled "Voltage,") time, transmitted signal and received signal.

If we were in a perfect world with the listed parameters; time, transmitted signal, received signal and there was no metal involved, the phase shift would be zero. Very similar to what's in the above picture.

There is one more visual representation that should be addressed in the above diagram. The transmitted signal and received signal are at different heights. This represents a strong transmitted signal and a weaker received signal. Just like when your detector transmits a signal into the ground and when it sees metal it is reflected back as a weaker signal.

What happens to our perfect signal when metal is entered into the mix? We get "Phase Shift" and this is the foundation of how the detector can "See" into the ground.

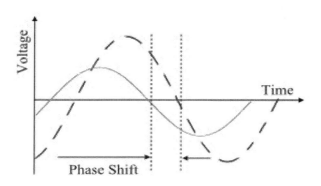

This is a grapghical reprsentaion of "WITH" Phase Shift.

This phase shift is the result of "Eddie Currents" that are created from the transmitting signal interacting with the metal. Each different metal will have a different Eddie Current, this difference is a measured time variable of the phase shift. These times are store within the metal detector and shows up on the display screen as a number, word or graph.

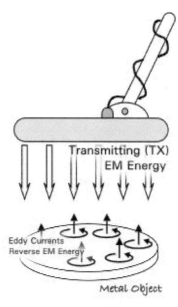

This is a representation of "Eddie Current"

Eddy current from steel such as nails or wire creates a very small phase shift, but things like silver coins have a very large phase shift. This phase shift (Eddie Current) is what metal detector uses to give it the ability to see different metals in the ground.

There is a spectrum of phase shifts, and phase shift increases as the type of metal changes and the size of the coins increase. Exsample of this is; Ferrous metals are at one end and large silver coins are at the other.

Sample of phase shift spectrum

The phase shift is transmitted and received through the use of two coils, one that send the signal and one that receives the signal.

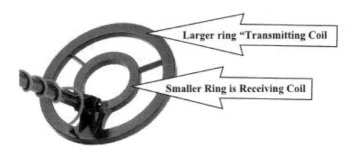

Two coils, one sends the signal and one receives the signal.

This two coil system is not hard and fast. There are different configuration and styles. But every metal detector must have a way to transmit and receive and it is done with two or more coils.

Coil Principles

The search coils is the part of the metal detector that is closest to the ground. It transmits and receives the signal that the control box uses to "see' the metal object that is on or below the surface of the ground.

Search coils include two or more wire coils, one for transmitting and one for receiving. These coils can be long loops of wire, very similar to how a cowboy would loop his lasso. The other method is a coil of wire wrapped around a core, if you could visualize wrapping a string around a pencil.

Both of these methods are used in modern metal detectors. The long loop style is mainly used in detectors such as the type in the picture below. The manufacturing process is done by dropping the coil of wire into a plastic housing; it is then epoxied in place.

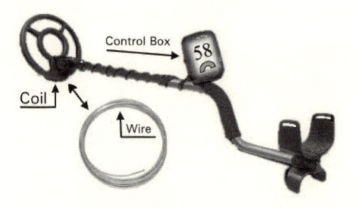

These coils can be long loops of wire

The method of wire wrapped around a core is mostly used in the small handheld detectors or pin pointer style, like the one seen below.

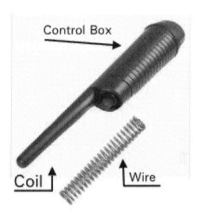

This hand held coil is wrapped around a core.

This information is important so you will understand that there is no one perfect style of coil. These coils come in many configuration style and shapes. They all have their good points and bad.

Some of the basic shapes are seen above.

The one thing they have in common is they all work off of the "Induction" principle and EM energy. We will talk about induction first then discuses EM energy (*Electromagnetic Energy*) next.

Induction

If it wasn't for induction, the hobby of metal detecting would not be around today. We as metal detectorist rely highly on the induction principles.

Below is the dictionary's definition.

Induction; *Induction within the areas of electricity, magnetism is the process by which an object having electric or magnetic properties produces magnetism, as an electric charge, by means electromotive force in a neighboring body without contact.*

The above dictionary description of the induction process is very staunch and rigid. Because it is a dictionary version, it is very accurate. But we as metal detectorist are more interested in the basic ideas on how this thing "induction" works. We want to understand our machine and the way it interacts with different surfaces, conditions and the items we're trying to find. Including the shape of the inductive field and how deep it penetrates into the ground.

"Without contact" is the key element within this dictionaries definition. Why this is important to our hobby is that we use induction in metal detecting process. We need this process as a way to "see" below the surface of the ground. Without the need to be in direct contact with the metal object.

One of the examples of this can be seen on YouTube and TV commercials. It is a way to charge your phone without plugging your phone into a charger. How this is accomplished is you place your phone on the surface of the charger (no plug to the phone is involved) the induction process charges your phone. It transfers the electrical energy to the phone without physically connecting any wires. This process is the basic idea behind induction.

The induction process charges your phone.

The process is basically the same, energy is pushes out through the coil (charging base) which produces electromagnetic energy, and this energy is collected by the phone and stored in the battery.

The difference with metal detecting is, this energy is reflected back to the receiving coil and processed in the control box, measured, compared to other similar signals and produces an audio or visual ID. This is all accomplished "Without Contact."

EM energy (*Electromagnetic Energy*)

The electromagnetic energy is the method that allows the induction process to happen. The electromagnetic (EM) energy signal is produced within the control box; it goes down through a wire, to the detectors coil. This coil acts very similarly to an antenna, although antenna is an incorrect statement, at least in the way that the average person thinks of an antenna.

Below is the dictionary's definition.

Electromagnetic (EM); *Electromagnetic is a branch of physics concerned with magnetism produced by electric currents and with the interaction of electric and magnetic fields, these field can be both Alternating Current (AC) and Direct Current (DC).*

Once this EM energy is pushed out through the coil, then down through the surface of the ground, it interacts with any metal object that is within the coils transmitting area. This interaction with the metal creates small circular currents known as "Eddy Currents." We touched very briefly on the Eddie

Currents in the Phase Shift chapter and to gain a better understanding, we will expand on those thoughts a bit more. These eddy currents produce a smaller reverse EM energy. This reverse EM energy is what the metal detector uses to give us a visual and or audio indication of where the object is and what the object might be below the ground, but only within the coils transmitting area. This area is very limited and is dependent on many factors that will be discussed in later chapters.

EM energy and reverse EM energy are not equal. The EM energy coming from the metal detector is overwhelmingly larger as it is being pushed out through the coil. The reverse EM energy bounces off the object becoming a small reflection (exceedingly small).

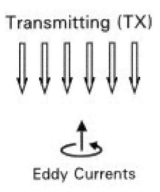

Signal Shape, Size and Depth

What are the shape, size, and depth of this EM energy?

If you could see the shape from the side, it would look very similar to an equilateral triangle. Looking at the shape from the front would be different depending on the type of coil you have on your machine. An example of this would be a concentric style coil would be the shape of a cone. Double D style shape would be a flattened out cone shape as you can see in the second set of drawings below.

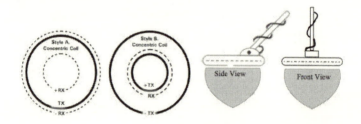

Concentric style is a cone shape, both front and side view.

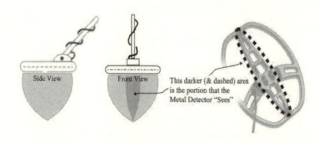

Double-D style this cone shape would be flattened out.

A good rule of thumb for the size of the field that your detectors coil can produce will be limited to the size of coil that you're using. What I mean by this is the field will not be larger than the coil. If your coils is 10 inches in diameter that will be your maximum width and depth. If your coil is 5 inches in diameter, the same will hold true, 5 inches in diameter and 5 inches in depth is max.

Depth of the EM energy field is affected by many things; coil size, soil conditions, moisture, conductivity of the object, mineralized soil, target, trashy ground, shape, setting, outside interferences, closeness to the ground, and even battery condition.

Ground Balance

To get a basic idea what ground balancing is, it is a variable setting that does not increase the detection depth in mineralized ground, but it cancels out the reflected signal caused from heavily mineralized ground. This gives the appearance of being able to "see" deeper.

Almost everywhere you detect there is some sort of highly mineralized ground or salty earth, such as in wet sand beaches as well as small iron particles that is found in the mountain areas and in red earth. These deposits will respond to your metal detector similar to how your detector picks out a target.

Because these areas are so large, most detectors have the ability to remove this particular signal so that it will find the targets outside the range of the mineralized earth. When we remove this mineralized ground with the ground balance settings, we remove the responding ground signals, so you can clearly hear your target and are not distracted by ground noise.

Keep in mind that every manufacturer of metal detectors has slightly different ways and methods of ground balancing your machine. We cannot go through each and every single machine and explain how to do each one but we can give you an idea of how this system works. They all have an owner's manual in which you can read the particulars on each machine.

Ground Balancing is a highly useful tool in your metal detecting bag of tricks. With time and experience, you will learn how important it is to ground balance your machine.

How often should you ground balance your machine? At a minimum, you should ground balance every time you change, moved to a significantly different area. An example of this would be going from a playground or park setting, to the beach. If you think about this, a playground is normally very hard pack soil, from all the kids running and playing on it, while the beach is extremely loose salty and wet.

Don't be afraid to reset the ground balance, it is normally a push of a button.

There are three basic types of ground balancing; manual ground balancing, automatic ground balancing, and tracking ground balancing. We will take a look at all three.

Manual Ground Balance

Manually adjust the ground balance setting, so the minimum amount of ground signal is heard.

Most of the times when we say manually adjust the ground balancing on your metal detector. We're speaking about holding down one of the buttons on your control box and doing a lifting and lowering motion (pumping or pulsing) of the coil near the surface of the ground. What this does is it adjusts sensitivity levels, which we call ground balancing of your metal detector. These steps and the pulsing motion will teach your detector how to eliminate mineralized soil.

If you are an experienced metal detectorist, you will use a combination of both automatic ground balancing and manual ground balancing; this will give you the best and most optimal results.

Automatic Ground Balance

The detector automatically determines the best ground balance setting. This is quick, simple and more accurate than a manually set ground balance.

It basically works similar to manual ground balancing as it was described in the previous chapter.

The difference is that the detector will keep track of the changes in the soil mineralization, and the type of soil, and then automatically adjust the value as you use your machine. There is no physical interruption or steps that you may need to do, it silently changes within the control box.

Tracking Ground Balance

The detector continuously adjusts the ground balance settings while the detector is in motion. This ensures that the ground balance settings are always correct giving the user maximum detection depth, eliminating the need for the operator to stop and manually adjust the detector as ground conditions change. The short version; the detector tracks the changes and adjusts to the corrected setting as you hunt.

No Ground Balance

This is also called preset ground balancing. Many very inexpensive metal detectors do not have any of the three different styles of ground balancing. The manufacturer of the detector probably has set the ground balance to an average value for all soils. The issue with this style of a metal detector is when you get in to wet salty beaches the ground noise will overwhelm many of the targets. This is one of those cases where being too cheap will cost you more than spending the extra amount of money on a slightly better metal detector. We have not found a situation in which this type of metal detector is worth using, we like a bit more control of our equipment.

Instructions for Ground Balancing

Manual ground balancing is one of those skills that improve with time. Once mastered, the ability of manually ground balancing will enable you to get the most out of your detector in any location. That versatility and accuracy makes manual ground balancing the preferred method.

Choose an Area to Practice

Practice on garden soil or something similar before taking the metal detector out to the woods, beach or other location. Make sure the area doesn't have any metal around. Stay away from fences, cars, underground pipes and wires.

Set the Metal Detector to All Metal Mode

On the screen menu or button controls, turn the detector to all metal modes. For nearly every detector, it must be in this mode for manual ground balancing to be possible.

Adjust the Threshold on the Metal Detector

You want to set the metal detector threshold so that it's barely able to be heard. So, if there is no humming, slowly turn up the threshold until the faint humming begins, and then immediately stop. If there is humming, turn it down until the moment that humming stops, and then turn it back so the humming can be faintly heard. Be as precise as you can.

Locate the Ground Balance Adjustment

The ground balance adjustment settings should be on a knob on the metal detector or within the menu on the LCD screen. It should be labeled as "ground balance" or something similar. The location is different for every detector, consult the manual.

Set the Ground Balance

Hold the metal detector so that the coil sits two feet above the sand, soil or other type of ground. Then, move it towards the ground's surface and take note of whether that faint humming gets louder or vanishes. If it fades, the ground balance adjustment needs to be moved in the positive direction. If it increases, the ground balance adjustment needs to be moved in the negative direction. Do this until the sound remains at the same level from air to ground.

This set is very important when searching for tiny objects, one that comes to mind is hunting for gold nuggets.

Small Gold Nuggets

Target VID Numbers

Target VID (Target Visual I.D. = VID) the whole idea and thought behind having target VID numbers is to make it visually easier to understand and predetermining what may be underground. Giving you an educated guess of what to dig or not. Keeping in mind that these target VID's are a generalization and they are not 100% accurate. A good example of that would be target VID number for gold, nickels and pull tab is all very similar. Each manufacturer is slightly different in their numbering sequence. But the overall thought is the same, using a numbering system to represent the Phase Shift of each type of metal. The types of items with very low numbers on my AT-Max represent ferrous metals and very high numbers represent noble or precious metals.

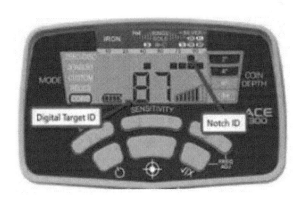

Above is Garrett Ace 300 VID Screen

The system is not perfect, one of the drawbacks of having VID numbers is that many times it shows nickel or a ring, but ends up being trash. The manufacturers keep getting better and better every time a newer model comes out. Remember this gives you a basic idea of what might be underground, not what is underground. The closer to the surface the object is the more accurate identification numbers are.

When you start learning this target VID and target tones, you should dig every item until you start understanding how the system works. One more thought about target VID's is that using a test bed and air testing is a good way to learn you're the VID numbers.

Do target VID numbers (AKA; VID Scale or Visual Identification) change as you swing over the object? The simple answer is yes, there are many factors that may cause a number to come up. If there are two items near each other, they may register one number on the swing to the left and coming back it may register another number. If you're swinging over a number and you turn your metal detect detector perpendicular, you may get another number, even though it was the same object. Here are just a few things that can affect the VID numbers; soil mineralization, depth of an object, ground mineralization, halo effect, more than one object, thickness are just a few. Many other factors can cause number changes including the position of the coin or object is lying parallel to the surface or is it at an angle or is it sitting on the edge.

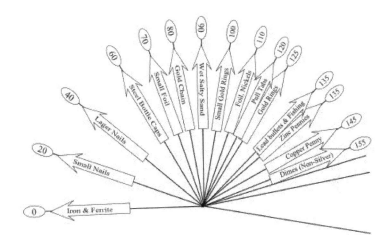

What if there is a large difference in VID numbers? An example would be; registering #10 one swing and you swing again and it registers #90, this is a clue that there's an issue, maybe trash or foil, even a combination of metals. If there's a small difference between numbers, jumps from #40 to #45, this is pretty consistent and you will have a fairly good guess of what it might be.

Another issue is you can have the same exact coin in beach conditions and that same coin in highly mineralized ground; you will get to completely different readings.

For a long time, the only thing we had was tone changes to determine the different type of metal. Once the metal detectors with target VID came into play, we were able to use both the tone and target VID. Giving the user an even great indication of what was under the surface. This was a huge advancement, and a very needed and welcomed innovation within the hobby.

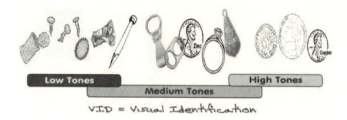

VID = Visual Identification

This target VID also gave us the ability to notch out specific groups of numbers. This capacity to notch gave us the ability to remove things such as ferrous metals, nails, wire, foils, and wrappers. Making you're hunting of coins, rings, and valuables easier to tailor your metal detector, and being able to fit to the criteria you wanted. Giving us the ability to avoid unwanted items and not needing to dig every target.

Features you may want

Features for metal detectors vary widely from model to model. What you should look for is the most features for the price range that you can afford. Your very first metal detector should have a few of these items if not all: a good battery source such as lithium-ion batteries or rechargeable may be best, a speaker with optional headphone plug, depth indicator, ground balancing, pinpointing mode, and a water-resistant coil.

There are many more items listed below and is best to pick a dollar figure and work up to that.

Think about how you're going to use the machine and pick the features that go with that style of a metal detector. This could be a coin and jewelry hunting or relic, possibly saltwater beach hunting and even underwater hunting. If you are looking at searching for gold nuggets, you will need to be sure this is part of the features that you want.

Audio identification

Audio identification comes on almost all metal detectors. You have a choice to have the tones come through a speaker or you can install headphones and listen to the tones through your headphones.

If you're looking for deep targets using headphones is a plus. You can hear minor fluctuations in the tones and it helps avoid outside noises.

There is a variety of tones that your metal detector uses for audio identification. Most have three levels, a low tone a medium tone and a high tone. The low tones or sometimes we call these "grunts" which tell you that it is an iron target or something on the lower end of the scale. The medium tones help you identify the medium-range items such as pull-tabs, nickels, rings, and similar items. The high tones give you the ability to hear good, solid coins tones; these include dimes, quarters, fifty-cent pieces and even dollar coins.

Built-in backlighting: There is a multitude of different lighting features for different metal detectors. There is one I feel is important, it's back-light of the gauges. If you hunt near dusk and dawn the back-light features used during these hours can be very helpful. The ability to see all the information on your screen, is a key feature.

Depth indicator: Most metal detectors with LED screens will also have a depth indicator function. This depth gauge (sometimes it is a meter or bar graph) is meant to give you a general idea of how deep the item is. If the item is very small, it may register shallower than if the item that is very large. Keep in mind that larger items could be down a few inches, but register only one inch below the surface. Plus, very small items may be registering very deep but in reality it is closer to the ground surface.

Is a depth indicator a useful function? Very simply the answer is yes. There are no if's, butt's, or maybe's. This is a good feature.

Ground balance

Auto ground balancing, manual ground balancing, preset ground balancing. Ground balancing is a must. There are several types of ground balancing, they are all important.

Auto ground balancing is probably one of the better features in the higher-end models. Once you get a good grasp on how auto-ground balancing works, you will ever go back to manual ground balancing. On most good metal detecting machines you have the option of both.

One of the positive ideas behind auto ground balancing is it gives you a little more control and accuracy over how the machine will act in highly mineralized grounds or salty situations.

Manual ground balancing (also known as all metal mode) is a knob or pushbutton that you would use to set your machine before you hunt. This process repeats multiple times as you hunt and the ground conditions change. Most of these manual ground balancing machines have what is called a threshold sound when it's in all metal modes. This threshold sound is basically a background sound or noise that the metal detector produces when it's in this mode. How you should adjust this feature is to set the level of sound until you can barely hear consistent pattern (you should get a very faint noise that changes when you are above a target) you'll know that it's fairly close to being correct when the sound is tuned out. It's that point of no sound and sound that you are very close to being ground balanced.

Another use for this manual ground balancing is pinpointing with your search coil. Hunt with auto ground balance until you hear a target, once you are close, switch over to manual and listen to the sound until you hear the loudest sound, both horizontally and vertically over the target. This will get you very close to where the location of the item. The loudness of this threshold would depend on how close, how big the item is and if your coil is located over your target.

Preset ground balancing is normally set at the manufacture and cannot be adjusted by the user of the machine. The idea behind it is to set the machine at a level in which the detector can function properly over a wide span of soil types and ground mineralization. I cannot honestly say that this is a good feature; I would not own one of these machines.

Headphone Jack Size: The basic sizes are 1/4 inch, 1/8th inch, hard-wired, speaker only, waterproof connector and one of the newer feature is wireless. I prefer the wireless style. The main reason is the cord does not get in the way when I am digging a target.

The wireless work via "Bluetooth" and is a good feature to have. Some detectors this feature comes standard and others can be added with aftermarket packages, Garrett Industry has a very nice one for a fair price.

Garrett Z-Lynk WT-1 Wireless Transmitter $75

Microprocessors

Convenience is what microprocessors have brought to the hobby. Most of the quality detectors require a flip of a switch to start detecting. Many have pre-programmed setups to do the different styles of metal detecting, such as hunting for coins or relic hunting. Most have the ability to do custom setups. These custom setups give the ability to fine-tune your metal detector to your specifications and not be stuck with a factory preset.

Things have changed a lot in the last few years. The microprocessors inside of your control box on your metal detector will allow for complex settings that can be chosen or stored. These microprocessors control a variety of items within your metal detector. These features are target identity, depth, battery strength, signal strength, threshold, VID number, and all this information is shown on the LCD display screen, to analyze targets and much more.

Probably one of the biggest advantages of having a microprocessor within your machine is the ability to do notched discrimination. This is the ability to accept or reject any particular style or type of metallic item.

This microprocessor can give different audio responses to the different types of metal. It can go from non-motion to motion by the touch of a switch. Cost of metal detectors in relation to what they do has come down dramatically, all because of the microprocessors.

Search Coils

The search coil seems quite obvious, but it is the part of your detector that is in the nearest proximity to the ground. There are several basic shapes and styles that we will cover in this chapter. These styles are Concentric, DD, Mono Loop and Coaxial; they all have their place within the hobby. We will touch on the different roles each have.

They main function of the coils is to send and receive a signal in which the control box generates. It serves as an antenna for the overall unit. This is the part that gives your metal detector the ability to see below the surface of the ground.

Let's get started with coil styles, sizes, and shapes. There are only a few basic styles, and these break down into two basic shapes. Concentric (a round shape) and the Double-D (DD's) of these two basic shapes, there are variations. An example of this variation is if they take the round style coil and change the shape slightly it could be an elongated round style. Each manufacturer tries to have a distinctive style, in which they promote. Many of these styles have no effect on the coils ability to see objects below the surface.

Concentric Style Coils (Round Style coils)

Double-D (aka: DD)

These different styles of coils may have cosmetic differences that have no effect on the performance, but give the manufacturer a way to make their machine slightly different. You might say they are trying to set themselves apart from their competitors.

Concentric Coils

The coil *(pictured below)* is considered concentric style coil. This style of coil will normally have two separate rings that can be seen, one larger and one small within the bigger coil. The outside ring is the portion that transmits the signal into the ground. The center ring is the receiver portion of the coil.

Concentric Style Coil (round or elliptical)

Concentric Definition: *In geometry, two or more objects are said to be concentric or coaxial when they share the same center or axis. Circles, regular polygons and ovals, and spheres may be concentric to one another (sharing the same center point), sharing the same central axis.*

This style of a coil is one of the most used coil designs in the MDing hobby. It is very basic and does a great job if you're a coin shooter, jewelry hunter or love relic hunting. This is the easiest to learn and is very common in your low-end to midrange metal detectors. This style of coil is the ones you can find in the big box stores. I do not mean this in a derogatory fashion; I have personally used and still own one. The learning curve is very quick; it's a great machine to bring with you to teach newbies if you're more experienced.

There are many cosmetic shape and styles which can be donut shapes, solid, web, spider web and elliptical in design. They all work essentially the same; the elliptical design does cover a slightly larger area with each sweep of the MD. The elliptical is a stretched out version of the circular style, very similar to the Double-D also called "DD" which we will cover shortly.

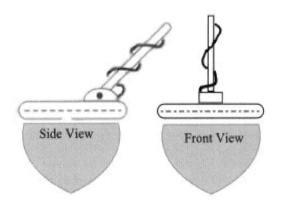

Gray area is the signal shape of concentric coils

Part of the design or usable area of the concentric style of coil is the shape of the signal (see above). It has a cone/conical shape.

Conical: *Having the form of, resembling, or pertaining to a cone.*

It produces a signal shape that is the same size as the coil then narrows to a point at its furthest detecting point. Very much like the shape of a funnel.

The signal does not go only towards the ground, but is pushed in both directions. This can be an advantage or a detriment. If you're detecting in a playground, it will detect an object above as, well as below the detector, such as steel pipes or play equipment.

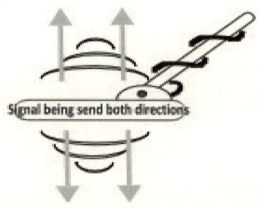

The signal is projected both up and down

One advantage that many seasoned detectorist assimilate into their practices is the use of the upper portion of the signal after the hole is dug and they are sifting through the soil looking for the object that was detected. The idea is to have the search coil near the hole and wave handfuls of dirt over the coils in an effort to sort and hear the metal object as it passes through the signal area. This is a faster way to find the object than to slowly move small layers of soil in the discovery process.

There are a couple of disadvantages to using a concentric coil style detector. The main one is the cone-shaped pattern of the signal. The operator must be far more attuned to the sweeping pattern, and this slows the coverage of the overall area being searched. If you are not being astute in your diligence, you could miss many valuable targets.

Why is this important to understand? When the object is deeper in the ground, the same overlapping pattern will not cover as well.

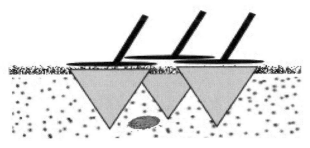

Overlapping pattern will not cover

But the advantages weigh in very well. I should start by saying if you're new to the hobby, this style of coil will pinpoint particularly well. What I mean by pinpoint is after you have located the target you can zoom in by centering the coil over the object for easier removal. It gives you a very precise location because of the signal strength when directly over the target.

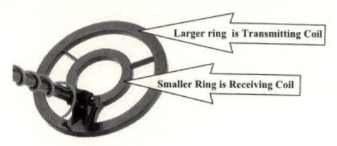

Concentric "Round" Coil

The nominal size of the round concentric coils averages about 8 to 10 inches. Once search coil gets above the 10 inch mark, they become substantially heavier and have a harder tendency to pinpoint. They also have a tendency to have a hard time with target separation. One of the advantages of having larger coil is search area covered including depth.

Target Separation; *Is the ability of the detector to "See" different object in close proximty to each other.*

Double-D (DD)

The Double-D (DD) style of search coil is a really popular shape. Many of the midrange to higher quality detectors uses this style of search coil. Most manufactures will have several sizes ranging from 6 to 14 inches.

The DD style of coil uses two overlapping coils; the searching area of this style is limited to the overlapped area of the coil. Each coil is approximately the same size. One side of the coil is a transmitter portion and the other side is the receiving coil.

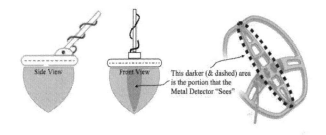

The dark area is what the DD Coil "Sees."

If you can use your imagination, you can see 2-D shapes letter back to back is why they call it a double the style search coil.

Double-D (AKA: DD)

A major advantage of this Double-D style coil is the overall depth and width of your search area. The diagram below shows the signal area that a DD covers. The DD covers a wider swing path yet a narrow target response field. I've also seen in some manufactures literatures that the Double-D is also called "2D Wide Scan." These two terms are a way for the manufacturer to be different; they are the same basic coil design.

Double-D (DD) style coil

Even with the Cost being slightly higher it is the preferred style of the more experienced detectorist.

One of the benefits of using a Double-D style coil is that it is less affected by heavily mineralized ground and trashy ground. This configuration results in an elliptical shaped (from the toe to the heel of the coil) sensing area which provides a chisel-shaped signal that covers the ground.

As you see in the picture above in the side view gets a nice wide swath with each swing of the metal detector. The view from the front is only about the size of the two areas where the DD's crossover the search coils.

The overall depth of the search coil is approximately the same size as the longest portion of your Double-D search coil. This style of coil does not require as much discipline when swinging the detector.

There is a disadvantage to using the Double-D coil. It takes place when detecting close to fences, rocks, trees and other object protruding up from the ground. The detection area is limited to the distance between the "seeing" portion and the edge of the Double-D. This distance could be a couple inches or even larger.

Mono Loop

The "Mono Loop" has both the transmission coil and the receiving coil wrapped around the same loop. The Mono loop search area is approximately the same as the concentric style search. In this style of a loop can be both concentric and slightly elliptical.

One of the disadvantages of this style of loop is, in a highly mineralized soil is much more difficult to ground balance. This gives the loop tendency to be slightly noisy. This will diminish the performance overall.

Coaxial Coils

This search coil design has the identical diameter transmit and receive windings stacked and aligned on the same axis: the transmit winding is sandwiched by two receive windings in near perfect alignment on center. This creates an electromagnetic detection pattern of more uniform density and performance and offers the best resistance to interference from high-voltage power lines. The electromagnetic field detection "seeing area" pattern of a coaxial coil is also coned-shaped.

Coaxial also known as "Mini Coil"

When using this coaxial style of search coil you have to keep in mind that it acts differently than the standard coils that you are normally used to. An example of this would be if you're using your standard 8 inch Concentric or Double-D the coil. It would transmit and then receive the same information on the top side as it would the bottom-side.

But in a coaxial style search coil it will's send and receive on the bottom side correctly, and on the top side you should get little if no information at all from your search coil.

Why is this important? If you were searching and found an object, and you use your coil in testing the soil by waving the material over the search coil, you should see almost no information or hear anything on the top side of the coil, but on the bottom side, you should get a clear signal.

This is one of those search coils that you should air test or bench test so that you will be familiar with how it works.

Does Size Matter

When talking about metal detecting, size does matter. It's not about how large or small search coil is; it's about how to use the correct coil in the correct situation. Most manufacturers will have several sizes of each search coil for their particular machine. Sometimes the search coils can be intermixed with the same manufacturing brand, but almost never be able to be switched within different manufacturers. This is due to how each coil is tuned to the machine. Each size and style will have their own positives and their own negative advantages. By having this variety of different styles and sizes, gives you the opportunity to detect in all situations.

We recommend having more than one size or style of coil. If you're an advanced metal detectorist, then more than one search coil is a must. If you have just started out in the hobby, then the search coil that came with your machine is a great way to start. As you progress in the hobby it is recommended that you fit your metal detecting skills to the correct search coil.

Smaller coils are awfully good in real trashy areas, the standard size coils are very well adapted to your basic treasure hunting, the larger size coils do well in areas with very low trash.

Mini Search Coils (up to 5" in diameter) - Mini Coils (AKA; Coaxial Coil) are just what they sound like. Because of the small diameter of the coil, we will talk about the negative portions first. The overall depth that the search coil can see is going to be approximately the same diameter as the coil. If you have a 5 inch round search coil, about the maximum depth is going to be about 5 inches deep. What these small search coils are good for is allowing you to put your search coil very close to metal objects, such as fences, steel posts, playground equipment, and very trashy areas. Another example is if you are using your metal detector in the crevices of rocks trying to locate metal items such as gold nuggets, then this small diameter of the coil is very maneuverable.

Small Search Coils (5" - 8" in diameter) - these smaller sized search coils, are suited for semi-trashy areas. They are also good in a highly mineralized soil or in areas where vegetation, roots, rocks and the like are much denser. Just remember that the overall depth of the search coil is in relationship to the diameter of the coil.

Medium Search Coils (8" - 11.5" in diameter) - this size of search coil normally comes standard, or should I say out of a brand-new box. They are basically coils that the manufacturer has dubbed the "sweet spot" when it comes to size, depth, sweep pattern, and will give you the best range of targets under the average conditions of metal detecting.

Large Search Coils (11.5" - 24" in diameter) – once you get above the standard size search coil, you do not necessarily gain that much more depth. After reaching the 12 inch diameter, there are many more things to consider such as mineralization, wet salty sand situations and many other items that will not allow you to detect as deep as the diameter of the coil. These items listed above are just a few of the negative effect you can have issues with and are much more suited to the seasoned metal detectorist.

Extra precautions – after getting away from the standard sizes and shapes of search coil recommended by the manufacturer, you must be diligent in readjusting and tuning each time you change size, shape and when conditions change.

Always use the proper search coil for the detector that you are using. Do not interchange search coils with different manufacturers and brands.

Submersible Coils

Submersible Coils "Wading Coil" - although these coils are waterproof, the materials which they are manufactured out of tend to float. In most cases, in shallow water, this is not an issue, but it can be tedious after long periods of time. If you have an enclosed loop *(covers on top and bottom)* the manufacturers tend to fill the inside of the search coil head with a foam material which causes this flotation issue.

Many of these manufacturers have what is called a "Wading Coil" and they have removed the foam and inserted a material that will compensate and create a more neutral buoyant search head. *(They add weight to the inside of the housing.)*

Submersible Coils "Wading Coil"

Types of detectors; quality, economy

BFO = Beat Frequency Oscillation

The Beat-Frequency Oscillator (BFO) is the simplest and the oldest type of detector technology. This style of a metal detector was once popular. BFO's are no longer being made by most if not all the better metal detector manufacturers. They're simple, inexpensive and don't have the accuracy, control, ease of use or many of the features in the new PI or VLF detectors.

Keep in mind that to enjoy the hobby you do not need an extremely technical or vast knowledge of this topic. To gain a perspective of how a BFO works we will give you a perspective on the basics.

An electronic oscillator is an electronic circuit that produces a periodic, oscillating electronic signal, often a sine wave or a square wave. Oscillators convert direct current (DC) from the power supply to an alternating current signal. They are widely used in many electronic devices. Below is an illustration of the basic signal patterns.

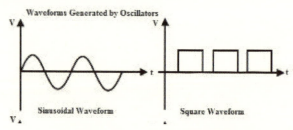

Two wave forms generated by BFO

Both the large coil and the small coil have an individual BFO, and they operate on slightly different frequencies, both of the BFO signals are tuned almost identical, but they are different and this difference is what is used to produce a signal within the control box that we can hear, it's audible. Keep in mind that this topic is far more complicated, but for now, we will stay simple.

Most metal detectors have a speaker that works with this portion of the metal detector so we can hear the signal when metallic objects pass within the signal field, this can also be a disruption within the signal area. We really don't hear the object that the metal detector sees; we hear the interference of the metal object interfering with the signals of the two oscillators. The circuitry within the metal detector produces an audible noise, this noise can be heard when the disruption within the two coils has been changed.

BFO style Search Coil

There is more than one configuration of coils and slight design difference, they are all one large ring and one small ring, and normally integrated into a single coil.

There are styles that are hollow in the center while other has a solid cover. The solid cover style has the same two rings and is for appearances, not design or mechanical reasons. The coils themselves do not need to be round, in fact, many handheld unit you see at the airport are oval to even rectangular. The principles are the same, one large coil with a smaller one inside.

BFO style Search Coil

The number of pulses or "beats" these BFO's produce is in the thousands per second. This is why we can swing the MD at a very quick rate of scanning the ground.

If you have a more scientific need and want to learn more, I would like to suggest reading "BFO Theory, by Carl W. Moreland, 1999." It is a 9-page document that goes into depth on how BFO works. His writings are very technical and intense so be prepared if this topic is new to you.

VLF = Very Low-Frequency

Very Low-Frequency (VLF) metal detectors have become the mainstay of the industry. The MDing hobby has had some great advancement; VLF is one of the most positive ones as a whole and welcomed this innovation with open arms. The usefulness of this technology has made it simpler to identify the targets below the ground, which keeps us from digging every single noise that the metal detector makes.

VLF detectors have become popular because they have become an all-purpose machine. They can be used for hunting coins your local parks, locating relics at your favorite ghost town and even combing the beaches for lost jewelry. Many of the better quality machines have submersible search heads that can be used in shallow water or your favorite beach. If you plan on doing any kind of water related metal detecting make sure you plan on this when you do your purchasing.

The majority of VLF metal detectors use a frequency that is less than 30kHz. Each manufacturer uses different frequencies to eliminate crosstalk *(this is when two detectors interfere with each other)*. On the higher-end models, many of them have the ability to shift their frequency slightly just in case there is two of the same model near each other. This helps if you and your friend have the same style and model. You can change your frequency slightly from each other and still get the same results with no crosstalk.

Almost all of these style metal detectors can give your proximate depth of the objects based on the strength of the EM field *(the Eddie currents)* that it generates. The idea behind it is, the closer the object is to the surface the stronger the magnetic field is picked up by the receiver coil and the stronger the electric current is generated.

But exactly how does VLF work? The VLF metal detectors have a transmitting coil and a receiver coil. The transmitter coil pushes a signal into the ground and receiver coil picks up this signal then sends it to the control box. The key element in this process is the returning signal is changed slightly after being interrupted by a metal object. It then goes back to the control box and is processed. The information is then turned into an audible tone and/or VID number on the control box the screen.

How does the VLF metal detector distinguish between different metals? It's based on phase shifting *(we spoke about phase shift in a previous chapter)*. Phase shifting is a slight difference in the frequencies between the transmitted signal and the receiving signal of the metallic target.

Because the small shift are so tiny it takes a good quality metal detector to process the information into a form that we can hear or see. This information that the MD receives is based on induction and resistance of the metal object within the transmitted signal.

Since most metals have inductance and resistance, very low-frequency metal detectors can examine this information then compare it with the different types of metal within the metal detectors memory and identify what is below the surface.

> ***Induction:*** *this is when your object conducts electricity real easy, but is very slow to react to changes in the current or signal.*
>
> ***Resistance:*** *this is when your object does not conduct electricity very well; its restiveness is very quick to react to changes in the current signal.*
>
> ***Memory:*** *Better quality metal detectors have a built-in memory of all the more common metals; it is stored in the control box and is non-volatile.*

In many of the better metal detectors will allow you to filter out or what we call discriminate objects at or near certain phase shift levels. This can be done in a couple of ways, by increasing or decreasing the threshold or by notching out a segment of a phase shift. This will cause your machine to only notify you when it detects an object outside those ranges.

Pulse Induction

Pulse induction (PI) is a far less common metal detector within our hobby. One of the biggest differences is that most of the PI systems use a single coil to do both the transmitting and receiving.

There are advantages to this type of machine one is their ability to stack or use more than one coil and make them work together. This PI sees a powerful and short burst of current through the coil of your machine, which is the EM field. Once this pulse is sent the EM field reverses polarity and collapses very quickly, resulting in a sharp electrical spike. This spike lasts a few microseconds (millionths of a second) and causes another current to run through the coil. This current is called the reflected pulse and is extremely short, lasting only about 30 microseconds. Then another pulse is then sent and the process repeats.

A typical PI-based metal detector sends about 100 pulses per second, but the number can vary greatly based on the manufacturer and model, ranging from a couple of dozen pulses per second to over a thousand. If the metal detector is over a metal object, the pulse creates an opposite EM field from this object. This returning EM field is different from the transmitted field and is compared to a sampling circuit within the MD.

The sampling circuit in the metal detector is set to monitor the length of the reflected pulse. By comparing it to the expected length, the circuit can determine if another magnetic field has caused the reflected pulse to take longer to decay. If the decay of the reflected pulse takes more than a few microseconds longer than normal, there is probably a metal object interfering with the pulse.

This sampling circuit sends a tiny weak signal that it monitors to a device called an integrator. The integrator reads the signals from the sampling circuit, amplifying and converting them to direct current (DC). The direct current voltage is connected to an audio circuit where it is changed into a tone. This tone is what the metal detector uses to indicate that a target object has been found.

PI-based detectors are not very good at discrimination because the reflected pulse lengths of various metals are not easily separated. However, they are useful in many situations in which VLF-based metal detectors would have difficulty, such as in areas that have highly conductive material in the soil. A good example of such a situation is a salt-water exploration. Also, PI-based systems can often detect metal much deeper in the ground than other systems.

Care & Cleaning of Your Detector

If you're like the average metal detectorist once you've come out of the field, the last thing you want to do is clean your equipment. But keeping your equipment in good working order is vital and it will prolong the life of your expensive equipment.

There are many machines out there that are NOT waterproof, if you do not know for sure, do not use water on any parts of your machine, ever!

It's a relatively simple process and many machines are not waterproof, so care needs to be taken in how you clean it. The machines that are waterproof a damp cloth works well on most areas. Be careful around any and all electrical connections and the control box. Be cautious around the LCD screen most are plastic and scratch easily. If you're not familiar or not sure if you're metal detector is waterproof or not, a dry cloth is a far better choice than a wet one.

After encountering the wet grass or near water be sure that you take all the extra covers and scratch plates off. This will allow your metal detector to dry completely before storage. Remember humid climates, rainstorms, morning dew can cause corrosion or worse rust.

When you store your detector for more than a short period removing the batteries from the control housing is a very wise idea. It will not only save you from buying batteries, leaving the batteries in the unit will have a very slow drain on them and will running down. If you get a bad battery and it leaks into your control housing, it could hurt electronics.

If you have one of the models that can be used underwater be sure to disassemble all the moving parts that may collect water. If you're one of the few that like to play in the mud, be sure you flush out all the cam locks telescoping shafts and wipe down and dry everything for storing the unit.

Saltwater is extremely hard on metal parts and most metal detectors have some form of metal on them. Using fresh water to rinse off the salty residue left on your machine is good as long as you do not use any type of high-pressure washer. A touch of mild soap goes a long way, never overdo it. You're trying to get rid of the salt and the grits of sand that are left over from the last beach hunting trip.

Warranty & Service

The information below gives you many basic ideas on how warranties work, there are also a few extra tidbits, and notes.

Standard Warranty

Standard warranty: This type of warranty normally covers the cost of parts and the labor to repair those parts. All the Warranty I've seen, this normally last for one year there are many exceptions to the rule. Most require that you send in a card or registrar the metal detector online. Yes, they will use your information for advertising.

Excluded models

Excluded models of standard warranties: keep in mind that when you purchase a metal detector and it is used in water that the Warranty is normally much shorter. If this is a concern, they may have an extended warranty that you may purchase.

Time to Register

Time to register: you'll have a limited period to send in your warranty card. Registering with your warranty card is very important. They use the cash registrar receipt to determine the date of purchase.

Ways to Register

Most brands will allow you to register online, on the phone, or via a postcard that is included with your detector. Many do not require you to register. The ones that do not need you to register are normally a very short warranty period

Transferable

Transferable: If you're thinking about purchasing a used metal detector, and it is still within the warranty period, be sure you check and see if this warranty is transferable. Many transferable warranties come with limitations, such as time limitations as well as types of repairs. Most of the time you get a dated copy of the original sales receipt from the original owner and where the machine was purchased; most manufacturers will honor the original warranty. If you are not sure, make a phone call to the manufacturer before you purchase.

Typical Warranty

The typical warranty requires all your basic mailing information as well as phone numbers, email address, purchasing information. Many times they will ask you a lot of questions on what your intended use is, where you purchased it, how you learned about their company and many other questions so that they can learn their customer base from the warranty card/registration.

Below is a very typical warranty, to keep them out of hot water. But the bigger brand names almost always will take care of the issue if you are reasonable and within the warranty period.

Typical warranty

Typical warranty: Metal detector company warrants that each piece of security equipment manufactured by this company is protected by the following limited parts and labor warranty for a period of 24 (twenty-four) months (the "Warranty"). During this 24-month period, this company will inspect and evaluate all equipment returned to its authorized repair station or factory to determine if the equipment meets this company's performance specifications. This company will repair or replace at no charge to the owner all parts determined faulty. This Warranty does not cover batteries nor any and all failures caused by abuse, tampering, and theft, failure due to weather, battery acid or other contaminants and equipment repairs made by an unauthorized party.

Filing Claims

Today's day and age most the time you will be filling out a repair form in a format that is normally printed out on your computer. Almost all the manufacturers are requiring you to print this out and send it in with your metal detector.

Once you sent in your metal detector along with the correct paperwork, you can request an estimate of charges so that you can make a decision if you would like to get it repaired. Most will take your credit card information over the phone. In most all manufacturers no longer accept COD. All shipping and handling charges are the responsibility of the owner of the metal detector, not the factory.

This is a basic sample of repair order.

In conclusion, the overall price and service needs of a metal detector can be at the high-end of the scale. The use of warranty and service work on your metal detector is well worth the little amount of time it takes to fill in the required spaces on your warranty card. My preference is to fill out the warranty card and mail it in, but I am old school.

Motion & Non-Motion

The main idea behind a motion style metal detector is that the search coil must be moving for it to detect an object. A non-motion metal detector will have a constant tone and when it detects the object, the tone varies. This variation in tone or loudness is a detector recognizes the object.

Most metal detectors today are motion style detectors that have an auxiliary switch which will turn the detector into a non-motion detector. Let's explore a little about how these work. Keep in mind there are exceptions to every rule, and each manufacturer will list their product and its specific features, and what their metal detector can do, including its limitations.

Motion Type

The biggest convenience of having a motion style metal detector is that it will run silently while you are swinging your search coil over the ground. It will only alert you with a tone or visual clue until your search coil passes over a metallic object.

Keep in mind that the only time you will get a tone or a visual clue from the metal detector is when the search coil is in motion. Although this motion may be very slight, it does requires a small amount of motion to be able to pick up the signal. When the search coil of your machine stops moving, so will the signal from the object that your metal detector is seeing below the surface.

Most of your higher-quality machines will have a "pin-pointing" switch; this switch temporarily allows your metal detector to convert itself to a non-motion style detector. When this switch is turned on, it will give you a constant tone which will vary as it comes in contact with the metallic object that is below the surface. This pin-pointing switch is particularly convenient to help locate the item; we will go into this a little deeper in another chapter.

Non-Motion Type

Many years ago, when metal detectors first came out, non-motion metal detectors were the majority and not the minority. The basics of how this work is when you turn on the machine, it will give you a constant tone, you will adjust this tone so that you can barely hear it. This tone will be a constant humming or buzzing. As you swing your metal detector and it locates a metallic object, the tone or buzz will have a variation within it. This variation could be a gain in volume or a change in tone. This variation in tone is what you're listening for, and it gives you a clue that there is a metallic object below.

This style of a machine can be used at a very slow methodical swing, even to the point of no motion at all. Non-motion machines have a slightly deeper reach, keeping in mind that non-motion is an "all metal" mode and there is no discrimination.

Pin-Pointing Switch

A pinpointing switch is a convenience added to a motion style metal detector. This pinpointing switch gives you the ability to change from motion to non-motion style metal detecting quickly and easily.

Ideally, you would like to be able to move quickly in a large area and once you have found a target to be able to zoom in real quickly and spend the least amount of time trying to find exactly where it is. The pinpointing mode allows you to locate the target accurately and recover it easily.

Most experienced hunters know how to pinpoint with their metal detector, it is achieved by switching from motion to non-motion, then slowly and carefully moving the search coil near and around the object that is below the surface. The pinpointing switch is normally a very easy to use, and convenient momentary on/off switch. The basic idea behind it is so that you can use this motion style metal detector, at a very quick pace and cover a lot of ground, until you receive a signal and you switch over to the non-motion or pinpointing feature of your metal detector.

In a later chapter, we will discuss standalone style or "handheld" style pin-pointers. The small handheld pin-pointers are extremely useful and we will go into detail in a later chapter.

Storage

Most of the battery compartments on your metal detector have a little rubber ring that keeps things airtight and water resistant. Between uses or removing the battery, be sure to wipe down the interior with a lint-free cloth and use a very minimal amount of lubricant on the rubber ring.

Try to avoid the extremes with all battery-powered devices they're sensitive to extreme temperature, heat, and cold. Just remember that most plastic items rarely survive an extremely hot sun in a closed environment, although the build these machines to last, mother nature will do her best to wreak havoc on your equipment.

If you're going to store your metal detector for long periods of time removing the batteries can be a very wise decision.

It's always good to keep your metal detector in a cool dry place. If you keep your machine in good condition and treated well, it will treat you well in the field.

Soft Case vs Hard Case Storage

There is no one particular way that is better than the other, the idea is to protect your metal detector. I personally have a soft case for mine. But when it is in long-term storage, it is out of reach of children and pets. There are pros and cons to each type of case. It really boils down to personal preference.

The higher-end models normally come with a protective carrying bag. They're normally very strong and made of synthetic materials and resist wear-and-tear. Yet they are pliable enough to wrap the metal detector and have a well-padded environment to keep your detector in.

Most have enough room to hold the detector as well as a few accessories. There's a variety of ways to carry it, many have handles while others have straps or a combination of both. The better ones have zippers that will go full length of the bag for easy access. A few of them have backpacking straps installed, just in case you need to hike into your detecting area.

Like with all products there are cheap inexpensive models and exceedingly expensive cases, but on the average, if you spend about $80, you will get a well-designed and well-padded soft case.

Hard cases for metal detectors are becoming less expensive and may be a good choice. Most of the big metal detector distributors no longer carry the hard cases. But I've seen modified cases from other industries used that work very well if you prefer hard case. Hard cases are recommended if you plan on flying to your location. The soft cases just will not hold up to the baggage compartments of airplanes. Protect your investment.

Backpacks

One of the major manufacturers builds a backpack that they call the tall backpack. It is camo, has a tool compartment, padded shoulder straps, a waist strap has several zipper enclosures and water bottle pouch. The compartment is large enough to hold your disassembled detector. The overall length is 27 inches and about 14 inches wide and has extra room for your accessories.

Before you purchase one of these, disassembled your metal detector and make sure that it will fit disassembled into the backpack. I personally have a metal detector that is 30 inches in length, and it will not work in any of these backpacks. I have modified a backpack from a sporting goods store, to hold my metal detector and most of the accessories I use.

They do make many very inexpensive models that they call string packs, do not waste your money if you are not spending at least $44 on your backpack.

Pin-pointers

We will be talking about pin-pointers which should not be mistaken for the term "pinpointing." This term pinpointing refers to the skill and/or attempt to align the center of the target with your metal detectors search coil. This is an effort to locate the item within close proximity so removal from the ground is easy.

These little metal detectors are one of the better inventions the industry has come up with. Yes, it's easy to get really close with your big detector and many people feel it is an added expense. What it boils down to is the less time it takes to find the item the more items can be found in the same time period. They are a necessary part of the metal detecting experience.

With that said let's take a look at what a pin-pointer is and how it is used within the metal detecting hobby.

What is a pin-pointer?

The average pin-pointer today is a miniature metal detector with a minimum range depth anywhere from one half an inch, to a little over 2 inches. It uses the same principle as a non-motion metal detector. It does not have any discrimination ability and of course, there are always exceptions to the rule. They all have a lot of features the basic ones are; submersible in water, LED lights, adjustable volume, low battery alert, belt mounted holsters, audio alarms, vibration alarm, adjustable sensitivity settings, rechargeable, lanyards and the big one for me is the ability to re-tune with the touch of a button.

There are a few very low-end models of these pin-pointers. I would highly recommend staying away from them. About the only thing that they have going for them is their price.

The below photo is the model I use and have found it to be a very reliable tool in my treasure hunting tool chest. But I want you to learn what all the different features are, so we will go through many of the important features.

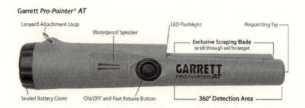

Here are the items that we think are important when looking for a pin-pointer. These items are suggestions and many models will have many but not all, there is no particular one item we feel is more important than the other.

Keep in mind that the purpose of this pinpointing device is to save you in recovery time. Think of these as a little metal detector that after you dig your hole, you can insert this small detector into the hole and get a closer look to where the item might be. Another way to look at it's, a way to keep the size of your hole smaller, you won't be digging a crater and in many cases, you can save the turf by keeping your hole small.

Bright color

The bright color on some of these is not because they wanted it to look pretty. It was for the times you set your pin-pointer down and walk away. Moments later you reach for your pin-pointer and it's gone. Being a bright colored object it is easily found.

Both vibration mode and audio mode

We feel that having both a vibration mode and an audio mode enhances your experience. If you wear headphones as most metal detectors do, the vibration mode is a needed feature. It will keep you from removing your headphones every time you pull your pin-pointer out. But there are times when you are not using headphones and an audio tone is best.

Lanyard

The lanyard or the lanyard loop attachment is a feature that is really useful. We use this with a retractable key chain that you get the hardware store so that when you're done using the pin-pointer you never leave it behind.

The lanyard you see below is an aftermarket item that can be picked up at most locksmith shops. They're relatively inexpensive and will save you from those, oops I forgot it, and keep you hunting.

Holster

The holster doesn't seem important, but it really is. Being able to easily pull out your pin-pointer and then slide it back in with little effort makes our sport easier and fun. We do not need to fight our accessories.

Auto-off and lost alarm feature

Automatic power off is one of the features that fits me very well, at the end of the day I forget to turn off my pin-pointer in this auto-off feature does it for me. The lost alarm feature on many models starts after five minutes with no buttons being pressed. They let out a small chirp to remind you to turn the pin-pointer off. This feature will also help you rediscover where you left.

Easy re-tuning

Easy re-tuning I have come to like. When you first discover a target, the area in which you're searching is quite large. With the auto re-tuning you can narrow the search. How it works, is you do a flower pattern around the object and what you found the basic area where it's at, you can push the re-tune and it will see a smaller area.

Flower pattern around the object.

You can keep doing this until you find exactly where the object is. It will also give you an idea of the shape of the object.

Tip detection, as well as side detection

All pin-pointers use tip detection. But many will have the ability to reach out on the sides the pin-pointer. You can use the side of the pin-pointer to sweep across your target area in opposite directions to give you a better idea of where the target lies.

Large easy on-off button

Large easy off button seems like it's obvious but a few of these pin-pointers do not have them. When a pair of gloves is being used and you fumble too many times trying to find the smaller buttons to turn your pin-pointer on and off, it suddenly becomes important. Frustration levels become elevated and it's just not worth using, check for large buttons.

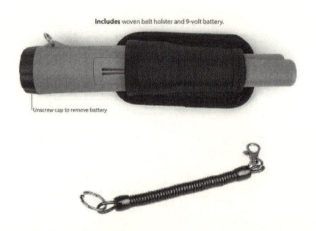

Pin-pointer Models

Below is a list different models that you would be able to type into your web browser. They are not in any particular order except for the "Garrett Pro Pointer AT Waterproof"

If you are going to compare any of the listed models, use this model as your base. We are not necessarily recommending this particular model, but this is the one that I use in the field. If I was to research for a newer model, this would me my control model.

- **Garrett Pro Pointer AT Water Proof: $150**
- Automax Precision v2: $140
- Automax Precision v4: $119.95
- Bounty Hunter Pin-pointer: $70
- Depth Master Super Probe: $120
- Detectorpro Pistol Probe: $170
- Garrett Pocket Probe: $120
- Minelab Pro-Find 25 Pin-pointer: $170
- Pocket UniProbe: $300
- Sun Ray X-1 Probe: $220
- Tinytec Deluxe: $120
- Tinytec Ultra Deluxe: $50
- Treasure Mate Pin-pointer): $170
- Vibra-Quatic 2 Pin-pointer: $169.95
- Vibraprobe 560: $120
- Whites Bullseye: $120
- Cheap discount store Pin-pointer $29

Low-end Cheaper Models

We did testing on several of the models, these were varying inexpensive one from a low-end, cheap, online store, and they did function. But after using it for a very short period the on-off switch failed. In the range of depth was from zero to 0.5 inches. It held together nicely for the minimal amount of testing that we put it through. But the overall consensus was you paid for what you got.

Our recommendation is to not buy a cheap pin-pointer.

Don't waste your money on cheap

Headphones

Headphones are not for everyone. Many metal detectors come with headphones in the box; they are part of a packaged set of items when you purchase a new detector. There has been a growing interest in using ear-buds instead of headphones. The higher-end metal detectors now have blue tooth, which is a wireless set of headphones.

One of the main reasons the average detectorist uses headphones is for the much needed outside noise reduction. This outside noise could be a lot of things such as traffic, wind, playground noise, even waves if you're hunting on the beach. Another real positive reason for wearing headphones is the ability to enhance the audio signal when you locate a target. When this outside noise is reduced, you have the ability to hear slight changes in tones that would be difficult at best to hear without good quality headphones.

In most of these headphones do not require any additional batteries; they are powered by the main control box. Has with anything there is always an exception to the rule. Several of the newer wireless or blue-tooth models have to be charged. What is important is the jacks size or style, USB charging cable or spare batteries. This is for those times when your headset starts to get low in power. It's best to fit the correct headphone jack size with your machine, by this I mean, if you use reducers to correct the size of the jack there can be interference of noise from a poor connection. Although I have personally used reducers so that I could use it ear-buds with my machine, I have found that loss of connectivity did happen frequently, although most of the time there were no ill effects.

I do feel that having headphones that adjust at the ear-piece, are far better than the ones that adjust at the machine. These adjustments are normally volume control and many models have both a left and right side adjustments. This is so you can adjust one side to be a little louder, if you need it, in case you have hearing loss or the headphones are not in sync with each other.

They do make inexpensive headphones; we do not recommend these. Mostly because of the lack of adjustability, but if this is all you feel is necessary, they are better than not having headphones. Quality in this particular part of your metal detecting gear may be worth the extra money you spend. You surely don't want to get out into the field and have a failure in this particular area and have your day cut short because of equipment failure.

Comforts is a major consideration, you will be wearing these for long periods of time. When buying, think about how they will be used, for what period of time, what will the average weather conditions be, are just a few of the considerations. If you have the ability to try them on that would be an ideal situation. My suggestion would be to go to a treasure hunting store, that will let you try out the gear, this is one time where buying online may be a disadvantage. If you don't have a detector store near you, go to a big box store and get a feel for what may be best for your hunting area.

With all the headphone choices out there, try as many as you can, think about the type of hunting that you do, and where you will be doing it. When you consider all of these factors, you will find the headphones that work best for you and your detecting style. Keep an open mind, I have both ear-buds for park hunting and when I go out looking for nuggets, I use headphones.

One thing on the positive side of using headphones is they will increase the battery life on your metal detector. Speakers tend to eat up a lot of the battery, but your headphones and ear-buds use far less and give you longer battery life. A quick note about batteries, always carry spares. It may be a pain to change them in the field, but it is far worse to walk back to your vehicle change the batteries and try to get to the place you just left.

Supplies

Having a backpack loaded with a lot of extra pieces, parts, and supplies, will make your trip more enjoyable as well as keep you out of hot water. What I mean by hot water is if you've ever been in the middle of the woods and forgot your roll of toilet paper, tree bark and pine needles are not as fun as it sounds.

Not talking about loading down an overnight backpack full of pieces and parts, it's about having the essentials for day outings. Small things like a couple of high energy bars, water, your cell phone, extra batteries for your metal detector and/or pin-pointer.

Water

Water is the first item on the list. Is relatively self-explanatory but how many times have you gone metal detecting and needed to swing into the local gas station and pick up a couple of bottles of water.

They make some pretty handy water bladders that you can attach to your backpack. They're less bulky take up a lot less room and hold quite a bit of water. Most of them have tubes that you can flip over your shoulder and take a swig anytime you needed.

It's also wise to keep a little extra water in your vehicle keep couple bottles full... just in case.

Back up Batteries

Extra batteries are a must, and you never have too many. If you've ever been on a hunt and forgot your batteries and had to spend driving time going to the nearest store to pick up extras, you know exactly where I'm coming from. Even though you have rechargeable and you can charge them in your vehicle, you should also have the regular ones fresh in a package for those just in case moments.

You should have them for your flashlight, your pin-pointer, as well as your metal detector batteries. Make sure that you have your charging cord with the correct adapter for your vehicle so that you can charge your rechargeable batteries while eating lunch or driving to the site.

First Aid

Small first aid kit may seem obvious, how many times you have gone metal detecting and needed a pair of tweezers to pull a piece of cactus out of your knee. If you're like anyone else that goes metal detecting there are always bumps and scrapes and bruises along the way.

Each one of us will think of first aid differently. But if you have Band-Aids, antiseptic cream, maybe a pair of tweezers and maybe a couple of prepackaged alcohol pads will go a long way in the middle of the woods or desert.

Weather Protection

Weather protection means different things in different areas of the country. In the mountains of Colorado it could mean items that keep you warm, yet in the deserts of New Mexico, it could mean both hot and cold. What if you're in Alaska? This could mean rain gear or heavy clothing for warmth.

You have to consider your area and where you are metal detecting. If your metal detecting in a park and your vehicle is only a few hundred yards away, then you may not need as much stuff. But, if you like to hike into remote areas than these items can be more complicated.

Weather protection is a very wide range of items and topics. It could be as simple as sunscreen and a big floppy hat. It could also mean caring a couple of extra-large trash stacks, so that if it rains, you can cut a hole in the top to stick your head through and be able to walk out of the distant metal detecting area that you hiked into. If it starts raining how about that second black plastic bag being used to protect your metal detector?

In my "go bag" that is left in the car, I carry extra socks, a warmer jacket, a couple of extra black plastic bags, plus a few other necessities as well as extras of items we've already talked about.

Cell Phone

Today cell phones have many features that in the past we used to have separate items to help us out in the field. Besides being a telephone I use my cell phone to take photos, keep notes, use it as a journal for metal detecting, it has a flashlight in it, GPS unit, compass, maps, and these are just a few of the items that you could use in the field.

Permission Slips

Permission slips are a worthwhile item to have a couple of spares in your bag. Especially have the signed ones from the old landowners. Many times you may be seen from far-off by an individual driving by and make a phone call to the authorities thinking something funny is going on.

Having the signed permission slips in hand when the authorities show up is always easier than going back to your vehicle to grab it out of the glove box.

There are areas that required you to carry a permit and having this permit in your daypack will save you much heartache from the authorities.

Knee Pads

Kneepads are a funny thing not everybody thinks about these, but when you're in hardscrabble or in places where there's a lot of sharp rocks, cactus, dried vegetation, and other need damaging items. It's good to have said in kneepads to make your metal detecting experience much more comfortable.

There can be a great variety of these kneepads available, from the hard stiff ones, to the soft foamy ones, and everything in between. It's best to visit your local hardware store and try a few pairs out that fit your budget.

Batteries & Chargers

Standard batteries (non-rechargeable) this is a viable option for many metal detectors. I personally use this style of a battery in my metal detector as well as my pin-pointer. They last a fair amount of time, the cost is not prohibitive, does not require a charger which allows me to carry a small package of batteries in my day bag.

Batteries are a personal preference and everyone

has their own thoughts and opinions on what is best for their style of metal detecting. The warning below is extremely important; I personally have had a battery overheat in my pocket. It is not a pleasant experience, so you must heed the warning below.

*** *WARNING* ***

Do not remove and carry a battery pack in your pocket, purse, or any other container where metal objects (such as car keys or paper clips) could short-circuit the battery terminals. The resulting excessive current flow can cause extremely high temperatures and may result in damage to the battery pack or cause fire or burns.

*** *WARNING* ***

Battery Storage

Batteries should be stored in a discharged state since they can self-discharge and may become inactive after a long storage period. They should not be stored for any length of time while connected to the metal detector. High humidity and temperatures can cause the battery to deteriorate, so these should be avoided during storage.

A battery that is not used for a long time will slowly discharge itself. Even with the best of care, your batteries should be replaced after 500 to 1000 recharges.

Battery Discharge Rates

Below is a diagram of the discharge rates of two different styles of batteries lithium-ion and alkaline. You can see that there have been vast improvements in battery life with the new lithium-ion style batteries. They will stay at a relatively high charge for a long period of time, until they get towards the end of their capacity and then it drops off very quickly.

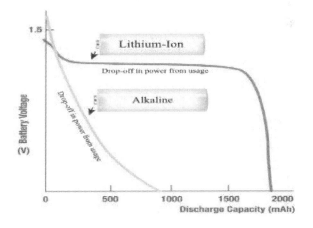

The alkaline batteries have a very steady drop off rate and with the availability of lithium-ion batteries it may be a good choice between alkaline, nickel cadmium (Ni-Cd) or nickel metal hydrate (Ni-MH) batteries in your metal detector.

Battery Chargers - Lithium-ion battery charger - Charging lithium-ion batteries is simpler than nickel-based systems. The charge circuit is straightforward; voltage and current limitations are easier to accommodate than analyzing complex voltage signatures, which change as the battery ages. The charge process can be intermittent, and Li-ion does not need saturation as is the case with other types of batteries.

You MUST use the correct charger for the batteries that are in your metal detector.

Follow the metal detector manufacturers as well as the battery manufacturer instructions when it comes to batteries. We take these items for granted, but they can become very dangerous if we do not treat them correctly.

Accessories

There are a lot of accessories a person can spend his money on within the metal detecting hobby. This all depends on your abilities skills and what you think is important to you. With that in mind, we will take a look at many useful accessories that could be of value, such as carry storage bags, harnesses, supports, extra shafts, wireless audio, stands, and if you're like me I feel accessories can make life easier.

Keep in mind that each one of these items we may have only a single picture of but there can be as many as dozens of options in this particular category or any other category, we have just one pictured and will talk about that one particular item to give you a general view of what is available.

Carry/Storage Bags

Storage bags come in all different shapes and sizes. They can be soft cases, hard cases in many combinations of this. The soft ones have backpack straps added to them. With room for your metal detector as well as a lot of the accessories that you may want to use on a daily basis. They come in different length, different thicknesses. Many have pockets, foam padding, Velcro or zippered, they can be divided, individual pockets or even one big bag.

The hard cases are a little bulkier but protect far better than the fabric soft cases. Most of the hard cases are made for your individual detector. But I have found that there are a few gun-cases from the sporting goods supply stores that work for a well. These cases can be adjusted by removing portions of the foam paddings for customizing. Most of the cases are sturdy enough take a lot of abuse. Many of them come with a key lock.

The photograph below is a Garrett camouflaged case, and we have added there promotional and advertising information to give you an idea of this particular model.

Garrett Metal Detector Case: *Digital camouflage #1616901 Padded travel/storage bag, 46" length with full zipper opening, carrying handle and backpack straps. Stow and go—Holds any current Garrett detector without removing the search coil! Five Velcro pouches to hold spare search coils, a PRO-POINTER®, manual, recovery tools, gloves, etc.*

Hard lockable storage case

Backpack style storage bag, this is the model I prefer for a couple reasons. The main one it is a virtual backpack, and what this means is that if you go backpacking into an area, that's off the beaten trail. You will look like an average backpacker and not attract attention to yourself. We're not talking about doing anything wrong or illegal were talking about blending into the surrounding environment so you do not create issues as you hike into backwoods.

Backpacks are long enough to hold your metal detector

Most of these backpacks are long enough to hold your metal detector if it's disassembled. Plus many accessories including your water and many essentials you may use during the day.

There are a couple of drawbacks and the biggest I find is the needs to assemble your metal detector every time you would like to use it. Until I found an item on the Internet that will allow you to keep your metal detector fully assembled but has a hinge in which all you need to do is push a button and the shaft will fold in half which makes it really convenient to pull out your metal detector in a short period of time and use it.

This product is called the "Fold-and-Go Kit" by Dan's Treasure Products. About the only place, I could find it was on eBay that range between $40 and $60 depending on which brand of metal detector you have. It comes in a bag with the correct hardware and fairly good instructions on how to assemble it.

"Fold-and-Go Kit" by Dan's Treasure Products,
NOTE: This photo is for demonstration. Metal detector and sling bag not included.

I found the first one was slightly difficult to install on to my metal detector but I have several of them and after that first one it was relatively easy to do. Takes a little common sense, but if you take the time to read the instructions, you should be okay with the assembly. I also used a spare shaft so I have one that is the standard shaft and one that has the "Fold-and-Go Kit" but I must say that once I've installed Dan's product I have never used the original shaft again.

Harness & Support

Harnesses and support systems used in metal detectors

There are several styles and types of harnesses and support systems used in metal detectors. Not all metal detectors need these harnesses, but the ones that seem to benefit the most from a support strap or a harness are the heavier models.

The price ranges from about $30-$130, and it boils down to the more bells and whistles you want on your harness or support strap the more it will cost. Many come as simple as a nylon shoulder strap with correct hardware to mount it on to your metal detector. Above is an elaborate one with shoulder padded and a waist belt style, it's a bit elaborate for me, but I do use the simpler model.

The idea is to put the strap in a position where it will hold the weight and be able to swing your metal detector easily without limitations. Most of these harnesses have instructions that come with them, many use Velcro so that you can get as close of a fit as possible.

The basic idea is to create the strap hold as close to the center of gravity as possible so that there's no actual weight that you're holding your arm it's all held by the strap or harness.

Shafts

Having a spare shaft could be used for multiple things. If you have more than one search coil it would be a wise move to have the lower section of your metal detector shaft pre-assembled to your extra search coil. It makes for easy use, quick changing and having a spare just in case you breaker damage your shaft.

Spare Shaft for your metal detector

Wireless Audio

Wireless audio to one person may be not using a set of headphones on your metal detector. But what we're speaking about his being able to wear a set of headphones and not having the cord going from the headphone to the control box. This is not a new product although it did not start until Bluetooth devices came along.

Absolute Easiest, Metal Detecting Guidebook

Wireless headset for your metal detector

It just eliminates the problems and issues of setting down your metal detector pulling off your headphones digging up your treasure. Part of the system attached to your detector and plugs into your audio jack, and it communicates via Bluetooth (wireless communication).

Many of the manufacturers of the brand-new machines have pre-installed Bluetooth within their system. But if you have an older machine they do make available Bluetooth headsets (wireless headsets.) Most of the ones that I've seen that are aftermarket come with a 1/4" audio jack. But many models of metal detectors have 1/8" audio jacks and I have personally tried the ones and used an adapter to go from 1/8" to 1/4" and I had no issues.

You do not need to purchase a brand-new metal detector with wireless headsets; you can get an aftermarket one at for a reasonable rate. One of the major online retailers has them as low as $65 up to almost $300.

There are several ways to attach them to your

metal detector. Most common is Velcro and sticky tape but many of these have clips that you can add to your rod or magnets that you can stick to the side of your control box.

Stands

Stands for your metal detector

The sales pitch that I see with these stands read similar to this, "Keep your expensive electronics up off the ground."

They make these stands in one piece configurations and are a little A-frame. Also available are high-grade aluminum folding units that telescope out and mount on the shaft of your metal detector.

In the parts of the country that I live, which is a high mountain desert, I do not deem them necessary.

If the stand is meant to keep your equipment out of the moist ground, dew, and/or any type of moisture and water, this may be a viable product. But for my area of the country, it is dry most of the year. I cannot attest if it a good product or not, I imagine they are in areas where there is a lot of moisture and water.

Shovel Holster

Absolute Easiest, Metal Detecting Guidebook

T handled shovel holsters

T handled shovel holsters have their place within our industry. They are made of a nylon plastic mixture for durability and flexibility of use. It makes them relatively easy to snap in and snap out your T handled shovel. The clip attaches to a belt or nylon webbing on your backpack.

Security Lanyards

Retractable security lanyards are one of those things that are very inexpensive yet protect you from losing a very expensive tool. How many times have you set your pin-pointer down and had to walk back and find it because you didn't have it on the next target?

They have a lot of different styles, makes, and models. You can pick these up from your local metal detecting store. I have found that your local locksmith shop has a few models that work very well and are inexpensive.

Two different styles of Security Lanyards

The ones that are made for metal detecting have a few accessories that go with them that make it very easy to mount these security lanyards. One of the models has a loop on the end which you would unscrew your battery door slipped the loop over the top and screw the battery door back down on to the pin-pointer. Afterwards, you would attach the retractable key ring to your belt or clips to a convenient part of your harness.

The product that I like the best is made by "Makro Pointer Retractable Security Lanyard, #1448-SL and suggested retail is approximately $20.

Rain Covers

Most of the metal detectors today have an assessor read that is called a Rain Cover. It does just that it protects you from the rain, it is not waterproof. It is basically a plastic cover with a clear screen on one side so that you can still you see the LCD screen on your control box.

Rain Cover

Most of will come with Velcro to hold it in place and the clear plastic cover stays fairly clear over time.

They are fairly inexpensive and they range from approximately $12 up to $40.

With any accessory, there are multiple styles, shapes and kinds of each individual one. The idea was to give you a basic idea of what might be available in different categories. In all the products and categories shown are for general knowledge purposes only, we are not promoting any single item.

Detecting equipment

You could fill a duffel bag full of accessories and extra items that might help you in your treasure hunting. The basic ones are pin-pointers, headphones, digging tools, sand scoop, coils, books, and the list goes on.

When you first start out metal detecting, you should try to keep your expenses to a minimum. Because if you're like most folks you start out with one style of tool and find that it doesn't quite do the job you were hoping for, you buy another. The most practical advice is to find the least expensive tool so that when you find out from use that it's not quite what you expect then you have not invested a lot of money into the tool. An example of this is digging tools, the small shovels that are available range from your local dollar store items, all the way up to spending $85-$100 on a brand-name shovel.

Even though the shovel is a needed item for the hobby, being a minimalist at first is a wise and proper idea. There are areas that you should be wiser in purchases such as a pin-pointer. Although you can purchase a pin-pointer at a discount tool company, in many cases a higher quality tool is a wise choice. I found this out the hard way by purchasing the cheaper model than purchasing a little more expensive model, and now I have a third model that is high-end and if I would've purchased the mid-grade one at first, I probably would've not of bought the more expensive one.

Pin-pointer

Pin-pointers range in price from about $40 to about $160. They have different features, in each of these features raises the price point a bit. I will be speaking about Garrett's pin-pointer, it is the Pro Pointer AT waterproof and its cost is $130.

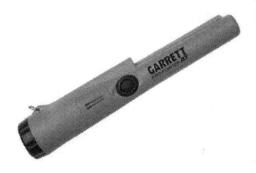

This particular model has the features that I prefer one it's fully waterproof up to about 10 foot deep, orange for good visibility. It has three sensitivity levels that can be adjusted on the go. It has instant re-tuned which is used to narrow the scope or field that the pin-pointer sees. This pin-pointer also features the "Lost Pin-pointer Alarm" and this feature is when you set your pin-pointer down and walk away after approximately five minutes it will admit warning chirp so that you can go back and find. It's a single button operation to do the power, re-tuning, sensitivity adjustment, and the stealth mode. It has a lanyard loop, a ruler, pouch, led light and a large power ON button.

Keep in mind that Garrett industries has not given me one or asked me to represent them, or paid me in any way shape or form. This is the pin-pointer that I use on a daily basis and I'm extremely pleased with, yes I paid retail at a metal detector shop.

Here's a basic list of the pin-pointers available on the market today.

- *Garrett Pro Pointer II (black)*
- *Garrett Pro Pointer AT (Orange, waterproof)*
- *Makro Waterproof Pen Pointer*
- *Minelab Pro Find*
- *Minelab Pro Find 35 Pen Pointer*
- *Treasure Products Vibra-Probe 585*
- *Treasure Products Vibra-Quatic 320 (waterproof)*
- *Whites BullsEye TRX Pen Pointer (black)*
- *Whites BullsEye TRX Pen Pointer (orange)*
- *XP Metal Detectors MI-6 wireless Pen Pointer*

Many models have lithium polymer batteries or rechargeable batteries, submersible up to 20 feet, wireless linked to your headset, up to 50 levels sensitivity, fancy paint jobs, replaceable shells, LED lights, low battery indicators, beep tones, vibrating, tilt on and off, tip only detection, VLF technology, fault signal, noise elimination, and pulse induction.

These are just a few of the variations between the

pin-pointers listed above. When you're looking for your pin-pointer should keep in mind that not all of these have all the different features. With fewer features, the cost goes down. Each and every metal detectorist has an opinion on which is the best.

It is up to you to pick the features that fit your situation and not somebody from a different part of the country or on a video on the Internet. Take the time to little research on this product so you will be happy the first time you purchase one.

Digging tools

The depth and breadth of this topic are enormously wide. You can purchase an inexpensive plastic heavy-duty prospectors scoop for as little as eight dollars and if you went to the dollar store, you could probably pick one up for a dollar, higher priced brand-name digging tools can get into $150.

Do you absolutely have to have a high-end digging tool, not likely starting out picking a sturdy small 6 inch long blade shovel and a coin probe preferably brass but it doesn't have to be brass, it could be an old screwdriver. Get an apron or a bag of some sort to hang on your belt and I like having a magnet nearby glued to my small shovel, as well as a plastic bag for the "good" finds.

There are many features on digging tools and a wide range of manufacturers, many of these features include double serrated blades, measuring devices on the blade, colored handles for visibility, sheaths having drainage holes in the bottom for dirt and water, lanyards, some are longer and could be up to 12 inches, some have zinc plating or painted.

But what is common amongst most of them as they are all made of heavy metal and are very durable, and most can be used for light prying.

Sand scoops

The most economical sand scoop is, of course, the plastic ones; they make a wide variety of sizes and shapes, from a basic large spoon looking scoop. The scoop shown below is approximately 12 inches long dark blue in color so that if a person is using it for prospecting can see the gold in the bottom scoop. This particular model is about a $15 item.

Light Weight Metal Scoops

If you step up in price to that you can get a saw tooth style metal digging tool for around $40. These are the ones that are on the metal detecting websites, they're not cheap copies but are well-made stamped steel that has hardened blades as well as a few other features.

Sand Scoop

The next kind up is what I think of is a "Kitty Litter Scoop." It's a larger version of the kitty litter version and has a big opening you can dig sand and sifted through the big holes in the bottom of the scoop. I've seen units as low as eight dollars at your big discount stores. They hold up fairly well in the short term.

Metal Sand Scoops

The next scoop is a more rugged and durable style scoop made of metal and there is a large variety of these. A few have no handles, just a basic hand grip. Then there are styles that have short handles in the range of 12 to 16 inches in length.

There are the ones that have the long handles which are over 18 inches long. In most of these are used on the beaches in the surf so they can reach down, not bend over as much and stay out of the water if possible.

They make them so you can buy your favorite style of scoop and add the size of handle that fits your needs. They make replacement handles and replaceable grips. A few metal ones are made out of steel and others are made out of aluminum the prices range from $40 to $150.

The higher-end models of these large scoops are made of aluminum and the handles are at least 36 inches long and with handles are easily removable. This gives you flexibility and you can use it with a 12, 24 or 36-inch handle. If they do not have a rubber grip on the end, you will want to have one. If it does not accommodate a lanyard on the end of the tool, you should probably modify your tool so that a lanyard can be used. The overall inside diameter of the scoop should be between 5 and 6 inches, the number of holes and the diameter of holes also make a difference. Very small holes and very few holes will take a long time for you to sift the sand through. Also, keep in mind if the holes are too large smaller items will fall out and you may need to re-dig them.

Probably one of the key features when looking for a sand scoop is if it can be usable in either wet or dry sand. Most scoops are riveted or welded, and I would recommend ones that welded. This particular tool takes a lot of abuse, with that in mind the manufacturer's warranty is probably a good thing to look into.

Shovels

Shovels are not unlike all the other products within a hobby. The styles and shapes features vary from product to product. Price range is anywhere from $14 to about $100 with features dictating price.

Folding shovel – The below picture of this type of shovel reminds me of the old trenching shovels used in the military. The handle unscrews, and the blade folds up, giving you the ability to lock the handle in place. The newest model of these folding shovels are tempered forged steel blades usually about 6 inches wide and 8 inches long and many of them have serrated blades for cutting Roots. Probably one of the better features that I feel is a good idea is the bright colored shovels which will help and you are not forgetting to pick it up and bring it with you.

T-handle shovel - This particular shovel is by far more popular than most of the other shovels in the metal detecting hobby. It has many of the features that are extremely useful and is very durable. The average length is about 30 to 32 inches most of them are painted black and the blades are usually about 9 inches long which is pretty much the depth that most detectors will reach. The better quality ones have serrated blades on one side; a few have serrated blades on both sides. Most have good foot pegs that are wide nonslip. Most will be the correct size to fit your shovel holster. There is one variation of the handle type; most are T-handle style, although a few come with a ball handle.

Bench Testing

Be sure to test any metal detector that is new to you, it's a valuable and needed process. The testing process that is done before you take it out into the field, has a few different names to basic names are, air testing, and bench test.

This process consists of setting your metal detector on the table or a bench, with the search head extended out over the edge of the table. This is so the search head is far enough away from any metal objects that it will not interfere with you passing several or many types of metal over the search coil. Passing this metal over the search coil would give you indications on what the signals and tones may be as well as how far away you can pass this metal object over the search coils, to get a feel for how deep the metal detector can see.

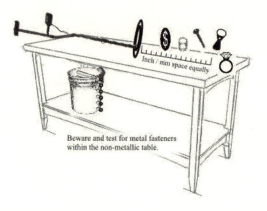

It's best to grab several or many items you may or may not be looking for out in the field. These items can be things such as coins, rings, bullets and jewelry. As well as items that may be trash so that you can understand both the tones and the visual signals (VID) that your metal detector will give you.

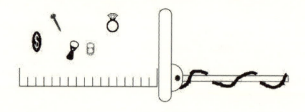

Metal detectors that give you a numerical reference (VID) can give you an understanding of the different numbers that appear on your LED screen. The idea behind listening to the tones and watching the reference numbers is so that you can make an educated decision on if the item is worth the time to dig up or not.

Becoming good at understanding the readings that are displayed on the detector will provide you and assist you with evaluating the targets. As the saying goes: "You have to dig a lot of pull-tabs before you dig gold rings."

Keep in mind that each metal detector has slightly different numbering systems, and this is done intentionally. The idea behind this is to keep you from going to a different manufacturer after you've learned and understood the numbering system for the metal detector that you are using.

An example of this will be one manufacturer may have a numbering system that uses the number 13 for a pull tab while a competitor's number would end up being the number 33. Although it's the same items, depth numbers and tones the manufacturer may change things a little to be different from their competitors. Keep in mind that these efforts are to keep you using their particular system.

Conductivity

How does conductivity help us metal detecting? When an object is very conductive electrical current can flow through it particularly easily. An example of this would be copper. In today's modern homes we use copper in our electrical systems because it is such a good conductor of electricity. On the opposite end of the scale is lead. Lead is a very poor conductor of electricity.

The modern metal detector uses this connectivity as well as the lack of connectivity (or resistance) to measure and return information to us this is so we can make an educated decision on if the object is worth digging up.

Depth Range

All metal detectors have two basic ranges. These ranges are the depth when you test the objects in open-air conditions (bench testing) and the field depth. The open-air condition is basically when your bench testing the object. You'll actually be able to register either visually or with a tone deeper or farther away under these open-air conditions. But field depth will be less depending on many conditions, such as mineralized soil, trash, or other objects nearby.

Below is a list of how conductivity is in different types of metal, keep in mind that this is tested with objects that are the same size and the same shape at the same depth. The below list is from the most conductive silver to the least conductive which is lead. An interesting enough silver is more conductive than gold.

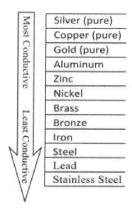

The most conductive is silver and the least conductive is lead.

Keep in mind that this is chart is for reference only, and that each machine has a slightly different and consulting your owner's manual is a must.

Metal Detecting Test Bucket

This is a basic thought on my idea of a test bed. It is a 5-gallon bucket; with PVC pipe at regular intervals up the side it of the 5-gallon bucket. How it works is you fill the bucket full of your local sand or dirt or if you're going to the beach use that sand. You have a separate stick or dowel rod with a coin attached to the end of it. You stick this coin into the tube and use your metal detector to test how each item reacts at different levels.

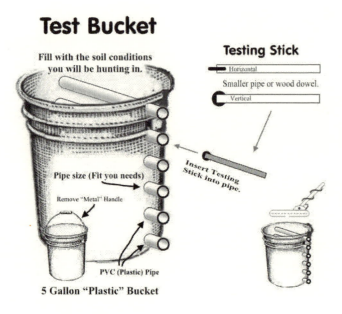

The bucket: This is a 5 gallon plastic bucket from your local home improvement store. The metal handle has been removed. We do not want the metal to interfere with our test bed. I did purchase the lid for the 5-gallon bucket so any extra parts I may have needed can be stored inside the bucket when not in use.

The PVC pipe: The plastic pipe's diameter is slightly larger than the largest item you are going to insert into the pipe. If your largest size is a quarter, you need to make sure that a quarter will slide into the pipe before you purchase it at the home improvement store. I also purchased a hole-saw that is the diameter of the PVC pipe, making it easy to cut out the holes with a drill.

The wooden dowel: I purchased several wooden dowels that could be cut up into smaller pieces. As well as cutting a slot into the end of the wooden dowel so I could attach the item that I was going to insert into the pipe.

The holes do not need to be in an exact size, but they do need to be slightly larger than the PVC pipe, they can be staggered, or vertically aligned like you see in the picture. Remember to leave a small portion of the pipe sticking out from the bucket. The hole does not have to go all the way through the other side of the bucket and neither does the pipe.

If you have more than one test stick, you can do multiple test sticks at the same time so that you can test how your metal detector sees a coin and a nail at the same time. Or any combination of items you wish to see. The other thing that I did was I use silicone glue on the inside of the bucket to hold the pipes in place. This created a situation where if I wanted to I could put beach sand in the bucket as well as add salt water to it to get a true or closer reading on my metal detector.

When I choose to store the test bed I just emptied everything, out dried it out, and put all the individual test items in the bucket for a later date.

Notes: I purposely did not give you exact sizes or exact measurements so that you can adjust to your personal needs. You can put the pipes is close together as you wish, or as far away as you wish and anything in between. The bucket does not have to be a 5-gallon bucket it can be any plastic, nonmetallic container.

The idea was to give you a starting block but not tell you exactly how to do it so that you could use what you had available to you.

Testing Garden

You should definitely locate an area and build a test garden if you are new to the hobby. This test garden, which we can also call a test plot, does not have to be a large area. The main idea is to have an area that is free of tree roots, rocks, excessive moisture, and away from electrical and telephone lines. The idea is to give you a better understanding of your metal detector. This test garden is a great place to learn how to adjust, understand, and work with the features of your metal detector. Inside this test garden you'll want to have good items as well as a bad item so that you can tell the difference between them.

Having the same item buried at different depths will also help you become familiar with your metal detector.

- **Scan the ground** - After selecting an area for your plot, set your metal detector to "all metal" mode, and then remove all metal objects within your test area. Ideally, you should use the largest search coil that you have available to you.
- **Select targets** - you should pick a few items out that you know will be found out in your area. Items such as nails, bottle caps, aluminum foil, brass ammo casings, a copper penny, zinc penny, nickel, dime, quarter, and any other items you feel is valuable to your learning process.

- **Make a map** - make a map of the area in which you're going to use for your test garden. Include on your map all the good and bad items so that you can refer to this map at a later date. Make a note of what the item is, how deep it was buried and the location on your map.
- **Distance between items** - a rule of thumb is to place each item a minimum of three feet apart. Once the item is been placed in the ground, you should have a marker of with the type of item and a way to identify the spot in which to bury your item.

You must remember that this is a test garden and not actual hunting conditions. When you get out into the field, you'll run into all types of conditions that you never expected. But using the test garden will give you a familiar tone, VID reading (Visual Identification) and it will also give you a good idea on the depth of objects.

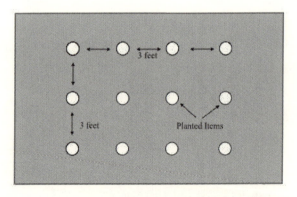

Test garden should be 3 feet apart.

Field testing

Field testing is very similar to test gardens, but they are a lot less formal. One of the ways that I like field testing is by attaching the object (an example would be gluing a quarter to a foot long piece of brightly colored survey tape) this gives me the ability to dig a hole in any depth I choose to bury the quarter either parallel to the ground or vertical to the ground. Also be able to easily recover the coin that I bury.

This may not seem so important unless you hunt as I do, and when I use a small gold nugget to test in the field, it would be very nice to get that gold nugget back, so glue the nugget to an object and attach a string or ribbon to the object. I purchased a big plastic washer from the hardware store and used some epoxy to attach the nugget and ribbon. It works quite well in my test garden and in field testing.

Don't confuse your personal field test, with commercial field testing. The idea for an individual to do a field test is to become more comfortable with the metal detector that they use on a day-to-day basis. Its functions, tones, and reading on the detector you use on a daily basis. It is not about evaluating one or more metal detectors for commercial reasons

It is not a necessary process to do all the different testing we describe here in this book, every time you pull out your detector. If you're comfortable with your metal detector and all its features, qualities and designs then jump right in and start finding those big treasures you've been looking for.

The big idea that we're trying to get across to is that when you run into different conditions, it would be a good idea to do a quick field test to adjust your machine before your day begins. An example would be if you had just come from a schoolyard where you are searching in the grass, then move over to a small creek bed, the conditions change and to quickly test your metal detector will greatly increase your chances of finding objects.

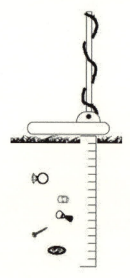

Signals; False, Good, Hot Rocks

Within the realm of metal detecting, we deal with and decipher different types of signals. The metal detector itself would give an extremely good indication of what may or may not be underneath the ground. There are many times when we will get a good signal, a bad signal, hot rock signal and we may get a halo effect on all the above signals.

With experience and learning our knowledge of the machine we will become greater, we will become more efficient and can determine what it's a good signal bad or a hot rock. It's a learning curve that we all go through.

Never become overconfident if there's ever a question on what the signals might be, your best effort would be to recover the treasure or trash, finding out what it really is.

There are many times where you will get a combination of signals in the same swing of your metal detector. You will change directions or move your swing perpendicular to the direction you were swinging to check the object below the surface. It will change from being a good signal to the bad signal and vice versa.

Good Signals

The first and easiest signal is, of course, the good signal, where your machine tells you roughly what the item should be and exactly how far down it is in the ground. It's simple, it's easy, and it's why we pay such a large price for a machine to tell us what is in the ground and how deep it is. It makes no difference if you are a beginner or a seasoned pro with the new machine. Digging good targets even if they are not a valuable target should be dug for a period of time until you have become familiar with the sounds, readings and the visual identification (VID) of your metal detector.

One of the main things you begin to notice is, you have a good target, and how is it repeatable. What this means is as you swing your search coil crossed the good target the sound will repeat itself at the same depth each and every time as well as when you turn it search coil perpendicular to the direction you were swinging.

Visual indication of a good target is when your detector gives you a depth and this depth does not change as you change directions of your swing. This normally indicates a good target. An example is if you have a coin that is 4 inches below the ground and you swing your coil over the top of it one direction and then turn your detector perpendicular, you will get the same depth and the same readings on your metal detector each time.

False Signals

False signals do not happen very often with the newer metal detectors. If you're getting a good solid tone in the correct range are looking for, it will be highly probable that the target is there. Many times in your digging you get a good signal but you can't find the object. This may be due to the depth, the dirtiness of the object, possibly within another object.

If your metal detector registers a coin for example and it says it's at 4 inches deep. You dig down these 4 inches and there's nothing there, it is most likely a larger item that is a bit farther down.

This is really not a false signal. It's more of a masked signal. When this happens numerous times, there might be a small cache or coin spill involved. Example: Your metal detector will register a single coin at a small depth, yet there is for five coins bunched together at a much deeper depth.

Hot Rocks

If you're in an area where your finding hot rocks, make it a good practice to dig as many as you possibly can. Many times these hot rocks may look like another stone but could be a meteorite, magnetite, gold nugget, a clump of gold covered in mercury (this is a case where wearing gloves is awfully important) or hardened black sand which is a material that gold is almost always found in or near.

One word to the wise, hot rocks should not be

viewed as always bad. This is because meteorites have a value that may surprise you.

Meteorite

Halo Effect

The halo effect is a situation where you have an item in the soil that is or near iron. This iron degrades with moisture. Basically, it's rust and as the item gets older and older this rust spreads out farther and farther around the item that your finding.

This halo effect will dissipate as you dig the item up. The reason for this is as you disturb the ground around the item that you are digging it is dissipating the rusty soil that your metal detector sees.

Gold should not ever have the halo effect; we are talking about the gold itself, not the surrounding materials that the gold might be in. The reason for this is gold does not corrode not even in areas where it is extremely salty ground.

Silver is relatively stable and most soils, it is resistant to corrosion, and the halo effect with silver is a much smaller area in relationship to other metals that corrode easily.

Copper and all of its alloys such as brass and bronze are the start of these corrosive metals, in respect to halos. This green soil around the copper products this is because copper will corrode with acid soils.

Iron products corrode extremely easy this is where most of the halo effects come and play. One of the new modern coins, the zinc penny has a particularly thin layer of copper covering over a zinc core and with even a small scratch these pennies corrode and create a halo effect that your detector sees a larger coin. What happens is as this halo effect acts like other coins. A few newer metal detectors compensate for this, but the less expensive models do not.

Keep in mind that different parts of the country are more susceptible to this effect in others. Areas where the conditions are desert like seem to have less halo effect than areas that are wet and moist all the time.

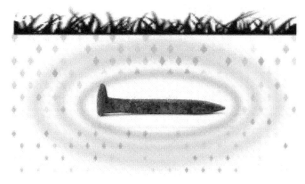

This represents the halo effect that your detector sees.

Tuning Manually & Auto-Tuning

Tuning History

If you're new to metal detecting and wanted jump right in, your success rate becomes more evident the more you learn how to tune and adjust your metal detector. Many metal detectors can be used right out of the box, but not all of them. To get the most out of your detector learning how to tune it is imperative. What we mean by tune it is, eliminate noise in the background so that when you swing your metal detector over a target, you can start recognizing the different tones that the newer models make. With a well-tuned machine, you can start hearing what the different sounds represent, quickly and easily. Let's take a quick look at the different steps it takes to tune the basic metal detector.

There is no substitute for reading the owner's manual, and if you did not get one in a box because your machine is was not new, most all metal detectors have an owner's manuals and they can be downloaded and printed from an online source.

A few things to think about are; if you using or testing this detector inside your home or building, you'll have to deal with nails, wiring, and plumbing as well as nearby metal objects. It would be best to start outdoors. Another common issue using a pre-owned metal detector is making sure that all the parts are there that came with the metal detector. Many times we have seen a metal detector come into our shop and have the incorrect coil for that particular machine.

Another big issue is making sure the batteries are in good shape; with weak batteries, you'll get poor performance. Look into the battery compartment and make sure there is no corrosion and the connections seem clean and visually intact. If you're still questioning the vitality of the batteries, take them to a place such as Batteries Plus. They are a retail store that has testing equipment to make sure the batteries will perform as you expect them to and can correct any issues you may have with your batteries.

When you first start messing with the controls be sure you take small incremental steps and it's best to work with one control of the time. These small incremental steps are so that you can start hearing and feeling and seeing the difference that each change makes. Many times you will be using a knob although many of the newer models now are using keypads. The advice is the same make small changes figure out what these changes do and how they affect the response to what you hear or see. Make notes if you need too. These notes should be what type of metal object is passed near the coil and how deep it can see, plus notes on the audio tones and VID numbers. It's always recommended that you air test or bench test your equipment before you go into the field.

They're a lot of terms that they use; a few of these

terms are noise canceling, tune, auto-tune, and ground balancing or manual tuning. All these terms are basically the same thing, what they are referring to is setting up your machine to operate in a range that gives you the quietest audio levels at which your metal detector will operate. Many of the higher end models have an auto-tune in them; this auto-tune will search within its parameters to find the point in which the features in the quietness of the operation are at its optimum point.

Most detectors before the 1980s needed to be manually tuned. How they did this was you held search coil at a fixed height above the ground and you turn the tuning knob until you barely got a sound which is what we call the thresholds. If you tuned it correctly this faint sound was barely heard. When the sound increased your coil had passed over a target and when the sound was gone, the target was no longer underneath your search coil. The motion was not required to hear the sound, this sound was considered drift. This drift would be affected by many things, such as temperature, the strength of your batteries, multiple targets in the ground, the height above the ground or even heavily mineralized soil.

One of the advancements that they made these models was push-button tuning. The basic idea behind this tuning was once your metal detector was tuned, as the battery weakens, ground changed or the height of your detector changed you simply push a button and it would re-tune itself back to what you originally set the machine too.

Each make, model and manufacturer had their own set of operating and tuning instructions which you will need to follow. Your first step would be to search online for an owner's manual, if you already have an owner's manual take the time one evening and read it.

Trashy Ground

The odds of you metal detecting on trashy ground is about 100%. It might not be this trip for the following trip but at some point in time, you will find yourself in an area that has more junk you wish to tackle. But there are always ways around you not having to pack up and go to a different spot. This did happen one time when I was out at an old baseball field. This was not an ancient field this was a field from back in the 1950s when pop bottles caps, the pry-off style, this was just before the invention of pull-tabs. This experience does happen and here are a few steps that may help out.

First thought

Probably the foremost is to screen out the iron and other non-valuable metals, such as nails, aluminum, bottle caps, foil, tin cans, and other such items. When doing this you are going to end up missing the extremely valuable stuff such as gold rings and many silver coins. The valuable coins and rings would be a great loss, especially if they are in proximity to items that are you are notching out. When I talk by notching out I'm talking about on many metal detectors, you have the option to "notch out" certain areas such as iron or aluminum.

Second thought

Turning your sensitivity way down will also screen out many of the objects listed above. Keep in mind that many times you will still get a signal from on certain types of metals that have multiple compositions. What this means is that you may have a coin and a pull tab next to each other and it will still give you an audio or VID. What happens is the MD will give you a false reading or a positive reading with a false signal at the same time. You may think it's a coin and dig up trash, but keep in mind that there may be two items in the hole, not just the one piece of trash that you dug up.

Third thought

This is a big one, the size of your search coil can and will either be an advantage or a disadvantage to your searching. A larger coil is going to scan a huge area and pick up both trash and good targets. Where a small coil, although it will take longer to search the same area, will give you a more quality hunt in trashy areas. But always keep in mind that your maximum depth the smaller the coil.

Last thought

Most new metal detectors have a feature which is called surface elimination mode. All this really does is it eliminates anything that is within a certain depth range. This feature does give you the advantage of eliminating a lot of trashy targets close to the surface.

How to Swing your Metal Detector

How you swing your metal detectors coil above the surface of the ground will make your success in the field either good or very poor. When you swing your metal detector, it is the motion that you use while slowly walking and searching for your targets.

It's exceedingly simple to make several mistakes and never even know the difference. A couple of the basic mistakes are the distance between your coil and surface of the ground. The closer to the ground that you can keep your swing of your coil the deeper it will reach.

If you're fortunate enough to be searching in grassy areas, you can literally lay the search coil on top of the grass. But in most cases, this is not an option. Where there are tall weeds, rocks, bushes and other obstacles you have to make do with this close to the ground as you can get. But in theory if you can keep your coil no higher than 1 inch away from the ground you're searching then you're in an ideal situation.

Another common mistake is having the toe of the coil higher than the heel of the coil. You can see in the picture below the correct swing is parallel to the ground. If you need to make this adjustment on your coil, it's a simple loosening of the spindle bolt pushing the toe or the heel to be parallel to the ground and then re-tightening the bolt. If loosened correctly, you can make this adjustment while standing in the correct position and lightly pressing the coil to the surface of the ground.

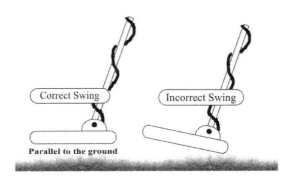

Another common mistake is made when swinging your metal detector and the raising the ends of your swing. Visual idea of this would be similar to a smile or a very low pendulum pattern. The idea is to keep your coil parallel to the ground. Keeping this parallel to the ground consistent will give you the best outcome as you swing your metal detector.

This pendulum style swinging will result in false signals and you will lose maximum depth on the ends of each swing. This pendulum style swinging will create a situation where many of the good targets will be missed by the careless detectorist. This is one of the reasons why we find many good targets at the "previously searched" sites. See diagram below.

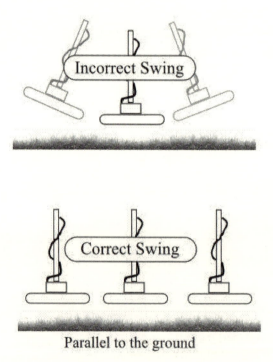

Parallel to the ground

Coil Overlap

Coil overlap is a simple and effective way of covering the entire ground without missing space or leaving gaps with your metal detector. Ideally the amount of space that you would move your metal detector coil forward would be 50 to 75% of the coil diameter.

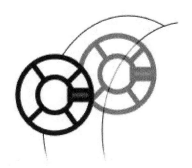

Over lapping from 25% to 50% is ideal.

Shaft Length

Your shaft length is a personal preference. But if the length of your shaft is too long and not adjusted correctly, the coil will be difficult to balance and cause maneuvering difficulties, false signals.

These false signals are not coming from the ground but possibly from metal within your shoes if the coil is too close, or signals being generated from metal that you may be carrying such as digging tools.

Crosstalk

Crosstalk is the interference that is caused by two detectors operating on the same frequency being in proximity to each other. Many metal detector hobbyists hunt alone. Crosstalk is not an issue for these individuals. If you belong to a club or go on organized treasure hunting outings, Crosstalk can be an issue if you have two similar machines with similar frequencies or the signal strength is high.

Depending on the gain or the signal strength of your detector, this crosstalk can happen anywhere between two and 16 feet. Many of the better metal detectors have frequency shifters. These frequency shifters can adjust your transmitting and receiving signals slightly, which will have enough change that it will stop the crosstalk and any other interference with your metal detecting buddies.

If you happen to go on a metal detecting hunt where there are many individuals detecting in close proximity, crosstalk is a real issue. The ability for your metal detector to frequency shift might be a big consideration in your purchasing a metal detector.

Best Frequency for Hunting Type

To get a good understanding of which frequency is best for the type of hunting that you're going to do must understand a few terms and gain a small amount of knowledge on these terms.

Metal Detecting Related Terms:

***Frequency**; When we talk about frequency in the terms of metal detecting, we're talking about the number of times a pulse or waves that go into the ground within a given time period. If we get a little more technical, it is the number of waves within a certain time period, which is measured in kilohertz (kHz).*

***Kilohertz**; (abbreviated, kHz), Unit of frequency, at equals 1000 cps (cycles per second). It is used in the measurement of radio waves, sound waves, and the like.*

Example of this would be if the signal would repeat itself one time every second would represent 1 Hz (Hertz). If the signal would repeat itself 100 times, it would be 100 Hz, and once it reaches 1000 times per second, it would be 1 kHz (Kilohertz).

After getting a rough idea on frequency and kilohertz, your question should still be. What is the best metal detector frequency? The answer is not simple, metal detecting manufacturing companies have been trying different frequencies for years. The problem is there is no "best" frequency. So far within the industry, there is only been ranges of frequencies. These ranges work very well for different types and styles of metal detecting.

Most of these ranges of frequencies are not adjustable. There is an exception to every rule. But the average manufacturer will have a set frequency for each different type of metal detector. Different types of examples of metal detectors would be; coin & relic style and gold type metal detector. Many manufacturers will have multiple preset frequencies. The exception to the rule is there are a few manufacturers of metal detectors that have a variable or multiple frequency style detectors.

If this last paragraph seemed very ambiguous, you are correct. This is because each manufacturing company wants to set themselves apart from every other company. They may claim they have the best metal detector within our hobby.

High Frequency vs. Low Frequency

A general rule within the metal detecting industry is a range between high-frequency and low-frequency this can be as low as 3kHz to as high as a 100kHz. Many of the metal detector companies choose a middle ground between 3 to 25kHz for the best depth and sensitivity. There is always the company that wishes to stand out from the rest and make an adjustable detector with a full range between 3 and 100.

High Frequency

The higher the frequency the more pulses, waves or cycles are created to penetrate the ground. These higher frequencies have a shorter wavelength which is better for finding low conductive targets such as tiny gold nuggets or small pieces of jewelry. The disadvantage of having high-frequency waves or pulses is the lack of depth that the wave for pulse can penetrate the ground.

A higher frequency metal detector also has the advantage of being far more sensitive to ground mineralization. It can also be more accurate when determining the different types of metal meets the surface.

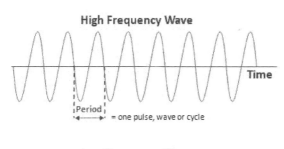

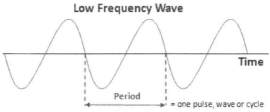

Low Frequency

The low-frequency metal detectors have a longer wavelength. This gives a greater depth penetration and works very well for higher conductive items such as silver. This low-frequency has a harder time finding smaller targets and does not work very well for small gold nuggets. The low-frequency style metal detectors are within the range of about 5kHz and below. This low-frequency can inhibit your metal detector when the ground mineralization is high.

Every year each metal detector company comes out with new models, styles, adjustments, and types of frequencies. You as a metal detectorist have a continual learning curve, and as you develop a style of detecting, your needs for a particular type of metal detector will start to narrow. Many times you will have more than one type of metal detector to meet a predetermined type of item you are trying to find.

There are beginning or entry-level metal detectors that operate on a single frequency as well as more advanced metal detectors that will have multiple frequencies that you can adjust or tune. The advantage we as metal detectorist have is as the manufacturers continue to outdo one another they develop better and better quality machines that become more affordable every day.

In general, gold detectors operate at higher

frequencies (to find small nuggets), while coin and treasure detectors work at lower frequencies for deeper penetration.

Metal Detecting Places

It's Logical, but...

Think outside the box. Stay alert to changes landscape around you, especially for those odd things that seem to be out of place. If you see an unusual flower that is not native while you're out in the woods. What are the odds that this was a flower bed from somebody in the late 1800s? Don't turn that blind eye, check small grassy areas, the indentation that is out of place. Keep an open ear to the neighbor that speaks about an old swimming hole that nobody ever goes to anymore, including playgrounds that have been gone now for 40 years. Look out into the open fields and admire that tree that looks 100 years old and wonder how many young couples sat underneath the shade of that tree. Start to recognize those unusual and odd situations that will reveal great places to metal detect.

Below are just a few ideas out of the many that are available, and hopefully, your list of places will start to grow within your journal.

Backyards – Start with your own, your friends, or neighbor's old clotheslines, tree swings, flowerbeds, porches, and walkways to the outhouse. Depending on how old the land is and the house on it. What will you find; Coins, relics, jewelry, bottles, coin spill or maybe a cache?

Fishing Spots - Many items will be sinkers, lures, fishing pole parts, pocket knives, kid's toys. Where people go, items are lost, and many times hidden by a young child.

Flea Markets - This is a place to find every type of item that can be found. Every place that sells things is a great place to find coins.

Beaches - Local beaches, town beaches, ocean beaches. There are many good selections of beaches on the east coast. Watch people and where these people congregate during the busy season. Imagine what you'll find: coins, jewelry, watches, and relics depending on location.

Swimming Holes - This is a great spot for rings. I remember one summer me and another treasure seeker found seven rings in at a roped off area saved specifically for swimmers at the old lake near town.

Parks - City parks, old parks, old ball fields, picnic areas, campgrounds. Look for - large trees, places lovers hide to get away from the crowd. What you'll find - coins, older coins, maybe jewelry.

Running Trails – Many of these have been overlooked. Detect the trails and any place where people get in and out of cars. Look in places where there are parking areas if they load and unload their equipment and prepares for the day there will be items to be found.

Playgrounds - City playgrounds, old playgrounds, sandboxes, swings. Look for - grassy areas, old trees, shady spots, unpaved parking lots. What you'll find - coins, kids jewelry, toys, wedding bands, watches.

Sledding Hills - These are great areas, has the individual bounces down the hill so does their loose change and personal items. Great place for coins, jewelry anything that a person puts into their pockets.

Fence Post and Rails - These fence lines can be feast or fathom and setting up your detector to discriminate out the old wire and nails is a must. Remember that any place a person works they lose items that include tools, knives, coins and the like. It is also known that fence posts are great locations for small hoards and caches, farmers and ranchers did not trust banks. I can't tell you how many pairs of glasses I have found near fences.

Property Boundaries and Walls - Back in the days where the banking people seemed to be more dishonest, individuals buried the money and used many places to hide their precious items. Places like; fence posts, near foundations, in walls, corners of buildings, just use your imagination.

Athletic Field - Ever play Sunday afternoon tag with your buddies and then get home to find out you lost your watch? That is just one item that can be found on or near these athletic fields.

Woods - Local woods, stone walls, foundations, cellar holes. Look for - new paths, old overgrown paths, search near the road, hiking trails, old wagon roads, foundations, old cellar holes. What you'll find - coins, bottles, relics depending on location.

Race Tracks - This can be deceiving areas to hunt, not only the normal place people lose items, such as under the bleachers. But I remember as a kid we went to the race track every Easter to hunt eggs and many times they put coins in those plastic eggs.

Fields - Old farm fields, tobacco fields, cotton fields, cattle, sheep, any farm fields. Go after a heavy rain, the main entrance to the farm, if you hit on a coin thoroughly search that specific area. What you'll find are prime spots for older coins, relics depending on location, artifacts.

Drive-Ins - Near where they served refreshments is one of the logical places to find older coins. These drive-ins were a big deal back in the 1950s. These are great places for old coins.

Riverbanks - Old marinas, old ferry launches, old fishing spots, old swimming holes. Look for - broken pottery and glassware, iron debris, old bridges. What you'll find – are prime spots for older coins, relics, buttons, bullets, sinkers, artifacts.

Schools - Playground areas are good just about every time you go. They are a consistent and good producer of modern coins and jewelry.

Amusement Parks - These places have numerous people in a limited area and are good for the coin shooter in all of us.

Even those the above listing does not cover all the places and items a person can find it does give you a general idea of places to get you started. Be sure to track what and where you find your items. It will be valuable in your future hunts.

Basic Rules for Permission to Hunt

Basic thoughts

Private property is not a stumbling block for the metal detectorist. It would be great if we could just park our car anywhere pull out the metal detector in start swinging away. At first, it will seem extremely hard to knock on that first door. Gaining permission is not only important it's also necessary, if you do not have permission to metal detect on private property, you are also trespassing.

Gaining permission is important to us as well as the whole industry of metal detecting. The more trespassers they have within our hobby the harder it will be for us to hold on to our freedom and our rights. Not everybody has the ability to get permissions from landowners; some of us have a hard time knocking on those doors and the thought of being rejected.

Foremost, leave your metal detector, tools, headphones, shovels, and digging tools back in the car. You want your appearance to be like you're the next-door neighbor coming too asked for a cup of sugar. Not a weird guy carrying an armload of tools ready to dig up somebody's front yard that was just mowed. The last thing you want is the owner's preconceived notion that you're there to tear something up. Keep your hands empty when approaching the property owner or his house.

When you're hoping to get permission from the owner, approach in a humble manner, you're on their property wanting to dig on their land. It will be in your best interest to always get permission in writing preferably, keep in mind that many people will not sign anything, in these cases, a handshake will work. Do not attempt to make phone calls to get in touch with the owner of the property. Think about the last time you received a phone call from someone you had no clue and thought it was a sales pitch. I personally cannot hang up the phone fast enough, so trying to get permission through the phone will cost you more time, than knocking on the door.

Use the sidewalk; do not cut across the owner's grass until you have permission to be on the grass. Even if you have to walk a little way out of your way, always use the sidewalk. If you see a "Keep Out" sign, stay out. Abide by what it says and save yourself any heartaches. This particular sign tells you exactly what the owner thinks of anyone coming on their property.

It is always best to get permission on the same day that you intend to hunt. There are many times when you have the opportunity to ask permission in advance, which is okay, but when you show up the day that you want to hunt be sure to go through the steps one more time and ask permission, make sure it's okay. Always be considered of the time of day, be careful not to knock on any doors too early in the morning, give people a chance to wake up and get dressed before you disturb them.

Instead, you should think practically: getting permission to hunt a site gives a detectorist more comfort and peace of mind to be more productive.

Always find the owner of the property you intend to metal detect. Never accept the next-door neighbor's, "I don't think they would mind." If the owner is not around, leave and come back another time. To determine the land ownership and obtain the owner's contacting info, you might visit the tax collector's office at local City Hall and find the tax records for a particular land parcel. If your search turns out to be unsuccessful, it will be up to your own judgment to decide whether to take your chance in metal detecting at this property without getting into trouble or go somewhere else.

Permission Slips

Should a permission slip be used? There are many schools of thought on this particular item. Many times a handshake is all that's required. But there are times if you feel funny about the situation, have a permission slip available. Something that both of you sign, this give you permission to be on the property and dig holes. Another consideration is to have the liability waiver form attached to that same permission slip.

This seems a little harsh but there are times when this is a much-needed piece of paper.

You could see a sample of this below and you may modify it to fit your needs and what you would like to say on the paper.

> **Permission to Metal Detect on Private Property**
>
> I, _____ agree to allow _____ to use a metal detector to search for and recover buried coins, relics and other artifacts located on my property at _____.
>
> It is understood that recovery includes the digging of small holes which will be repaired as nearly as possible to original condition. This permission will remain in effect until such time that it is revoked in writing.
>
> _____ (Signature) _____ (Date)
>
> **Liability Waiver Form**
>
> In consideration of permission to use a metal detector to search for and recover metal artifacts on the property located at _____ and owned by _____, _____, agree to release from all liability for personal injury or property damage that I may suffer as the result of my searching said property. This release is binding and discharges said owner, his or her heirs, executors, administrators, from all actions, causes of action, claims and demands for, upon, or by reason of any damage, loss, injury which I may sustain while engaged in metal detecting on the owner's property.
>
> _____ (Signature)
> _____ (Address)
> _____ (Date)
>
> NOTES:
>
> *SAMPLE ONLY*

Be sure you abide by the piece of paper both of you have signed, and if the owner feels that there are other limitations that need to be in writing. Be sure to write it on the paper and both of you initial that same paper.

The above permission slip is a sample of style that you should use. I would recommend that you consult your attorney if you want a legal document.

Here are a few more items that you may want or not want in your permission slip.

The Detectorist Code of Ethics:

I WILL NOT litter and I will always pack out the trash and dispose of all trash found.

I WILL leave all gates and other accesses to land as found.

I WILL NOT damage natural resources, wildlife habitats, or any private property.

I WILL use thoughtfulness, consideration, and courtesy at all times.

I WILL always check federal, state, county and local laws before searching. It is my responsibility to "Know the Law".

I WILL respect private property and will not enter private property without the owner's permission. Where possible, such permission will be in writing.

I WILL take care to refill all holes and not leave any damage.

Grid Searching

Grid Searching Basics

The basic idea behind grid searching is taking it a large area and breaking it down into smaller zones and then using those zones to search small portions. This gives an advantage of not going over the same area twice or missing sections that may be of importance.

If you can imagine a football field, ideally to search the football field would be to follow the grid lines. You would take one yardage such as the 10 yard line and complete the whole line and then move over about the width of your swing and go the opposite direction and you would can they continue that doing this until the whole field was done.

If you wanted to be extreme, you would go perpendicular to the yards marking lines. Continue until you've searched the field a second time.

In many cases where we have looked for jewelry in a specific area for an individual who lost it, we would map out the section good follow that line completely and then turn around and go the opposite following the same line so that we would get double coverage and not miss anything

String Lines

This is where you would take a rather large role twine and a few stakes and you would put a stake in the ground stretch out the line and follow that line and then move over a few feet and repeat. It keeps you from going in an erratic direction.

Chain Dragging

Chain dragging is an unusual but effective method of grid searching. The idea is to tie a chain on a rope behind you as you metal detect it will leave a pattern or a trail of where you have been. This gives you the opportunity to know exactly where you were and where you can go without constantly metal detecting the same places you've done before. In dry desert areas, this chain dragging works very well because it leaves easily seen marks in the sand.

GPS Positioning

If you have the availability of using GPS on your phone, this may be of interest to you, it will give you the opportunity to know exactly where you been, the same day year there, as well as on days in the past. We are not endorsing this product but this will give you an idea of one of the apps of the many that are available, and its location at the bottom of the description.

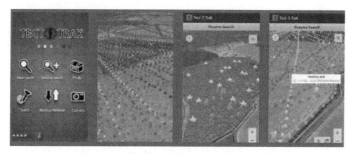

Tect-O-Trak is an Android GPS tracking and finds recording application.

Specifically designed for the metal detectorist, by a detectorist. This application allows the user to track and record their movements within a pre-defined area. Searches can be saved and resumed. Additionally, you can also mark/ revisits find spots, and make detailed photo and text records of your finds. You can also view and interact with your files on Google Earth using the KML export tool. For detailed instructions on how to use Tect-O-Trak,

http://historyhunters.co.uk/tectotrak/

Proper Digging Techniques

What exactly is probing?

Probing is the use of a thin rod in which you push into the ground to locate the item that your metal detector has targeted. There are two basic styles of probes, brass, and steel. Both of these styles are very similar to a screwdriver. The better models come with a plastic handle with the lanyard attached, approximately 6 inches long and on the end, it has a rounded point, but not sharp. Each one of these types of probes has pros and cons. They are both used with the same techniques and methods.

Brass probe

Brass probes are less likely to damage the item that you seek below the surface of the ground. This is because they are made of a softer metal, then the items that you are probing for. The biggest drawback of using a brass probe is that this tool will bend easily when using it for prying.

Steel probe

Steel probes also have drawbacks, the biggest one is when you are searching for valuable coins and items, the likelihood of damaging the item would be extremely high. The positive side is that the tool would last much longer and could be thinner in diameter.

Basic Method

Let's take a look at how it's done. After locating the target with your metal detector, narrow the area of discovery with your pin-pointer. You will then use the probe as a secondary locating tool.

By slowly pushing your tool into the ground, you will feel the resistance of the object that you have located. By sliding your finger down along the tool until it touches the ground, and holding your finger in place, you can judge the depth of your item by looking at the probe.

The next step would be to move the probe over to the edge of the target. This may take several tries depending on how large the object is, each time pushing the probe into the ground, until it pushes in at a deeper depth. Once you reach this deeper depth, it will tell you where the edge of the target.

Once you find the edge of your target, go slightly below the target. Use the probe as a pry bar; gently lift up the object to the surface of the grass.

Advanced uses of your probe are to puncture several holes to loosen the soil all around the object so when you pry it comes up easier.

Another method is to push the probe almost all the way down to the object, then lift the probe up slightly and rotated in a circle to disrupt the soil so that when you use the probe to pry up the object, the object comes to the surface easier.

Remember to repair the area of the sod and/or lawn where you did your target removal.

Conclusion

Probing is most successfully done when it is anywhere between zero and 4 inches below the surface, much deeper than that and it is very hard to remove the object with your tool. It's not an easy method but after practice, you'll become efficient enough that you may use this particular method in well-groomed lawns.

The Technique of Plugging

The plugging method can be damaging to well-groomed lawns. Plugging can consist of very small 2 inch holes all the way up to a shovel size. It is recommended that plugging should be done in a naturally wooded areas and fields. But very limited use in grassy park areas or lawns. It may look okay when you first leave the area. Your intentions are to not harm anything, if plugging is not done very precisely it will damage the turf, leaving a yellow "dead" spot that will remain long after you leave. This one thing within itself leaves terrible images of our hobby and creates bad vibes amongst the individuals in which we would like to work with searching their property.

Basic Method

After pinpointing the target, cut (using a digger or a sturdy blade) a half-moon shaped plug, 4-5" deep and 2-5" in diameter, around the center of your target. Cut straight down into the ground, but leave the one side of the plug attached. Cutting a hinged plug rather than an entire "plate" will properly orient its return, prevent removal by a lawnmower and lessen the chance of scratching your target. Most importantly it will allow the root system of the plug to remain intact, keeping the plug alive and green.

Once cut, insert your knife or digger down opposite the hinge and carefully fold it back. Scan the plug and the hole to isolate the target location. If the target is in the plug, carefully probe until located, and carefully extract to minimize damage to roots and plug integrity. If the target is still in the hole and not visible, use a hand held pin-pointer or probe the bottom and sides of the hole until the target is located and removed. If you need to remove more dirt from the hole, carefully collect it on a rag or small tarp patch so it can be returned to the hole when finished.

By placing any dirt on a cloth, it will keep the site clean and make it much easier to return to the hole. Replace all loose dirt with the plug, seat firmly and press it down with your foot to remove any air pockets. Done properly, you will leave no trace and the grass will remain healthy.

Conclusion

If you feel that your plugging method is sound. Cut a few plugs in your own front lawn and watch to see if they turn yellow and die.

If you can do any method that will not harm the lawn, do that method first, before you cut a plug in a manicured lawn. All it takes is one individual to screw things up for the whole hobby.

Electrical Interference

All metal detectors, regardless of the brand name, model, or even the age of your metal detector. They are all susceptible to electrical interference. There are two basic types of electrical interference, man-made and natural sources. Electromagnetic interference (EMI), also called radio-frequency interference (RFI) when in the radio frequency spectrum, is a disturbance generated by an external source that affects an electrical circuit.

Exactly what is electrical interference?

EMI (electromagnetic interference) is the disruption of operation of an electronic device when it is in the vicinity of an electromagnetic field (EM field).

An example of this is the fluorescent lights indoors. The older fluorescent lights you can hear a buzz when they start to get old and worn and this will wreak havoc on your metal detector. I realize that you will probably never use your metal detector indoors except for air/bench testing. Possibly when you go into a large box store purchase a metal detector and they have a sample that you can use or test. But these florescent lights make it seem like it is hard to adjust. This new metal detector is, in fact, having issues and it's the lights, not the metal detector that's causing the issue.

Outside type of electrical interference could be overhead power lines, underground power lines, and an unusual one is baby monitors, and if you are metal detecting in or near someone's home and they have a baby monitor inside this may cause issues in your metal detecting settings.

A few thoughts on natural occurring electrical interference are solar flares and the northern lights. These are less common than the man-made ones, these odd interferences still need to be considered if you're metal detecting on a day where solar activity is at a peak.

Any electronic device can potentially create interference. Wireless devices such as cell phones tend to be prone to generating electromagnetic interference although it may be small if your cell phone is really close to your metal detector it may be responsible for the interference.

Adjusting out EMI's and RFI's

The basic use of sensitivity control is to help eliminate electromagnetic interference (EMI). One of the most common ways to determine if you are getting EMI's is if you're holding your metal detector search coil steady and you still get an erratic beeping or tones. You are probably near some type of EMI.

By reducing the sensitivity on your control box of your metal detector will help with these EMI interferences. Be sure to consult your owner's manual they will most likely have a section on this particular item which you will encounter on a semi-regular basis.

One other thought if you go metal detecting with a friend or group its best to keep approximately 20 feet away from each other. This will reduce the EMI between the machines.

Pin Pointing (with your detector)

Pinpointing with your metal detector is probably the second most used skill that you will learn. It is a skill that is used almost every time you find a target. If you are a seasoned pro, it's the skill you use and are accustomed to, you don't even think of it as a skill.

Pinpointing with your metal detector is the process of narrowing the scope or the area in which you will need to dig. Most metal detectors are set up for full-motion and have a simple and easy pushbutton to go to all metal mode or a few manufacturers call it a pinpointing mode. This pinpointing mode is a temporary push button hold, so you can narrow the field and limit the amount of the area that you will get a tone or reading on your LED screen.

In essence when we pinpoint you are aligning the center of the targets response area to the center of your search coil.

Use your detector in both directions (perpendicular) to get even closer.

Each detector's instruction manual includes a how-to description of pinpointing technique and explains the use of pinpointing modes.

Where pinpointing is highly recommended and used most often is on lawns, this is so you do not disturb, damage manicured areas of grass. This is where a small hole is very valuable. Unlike working in a wooded area where a large hole dug with a shovel is relatively acceptable.

Pinpointing will also help in areas where there is a large amount of scrap and junk, and you would like to narrow the area in which is excavated.

Pinpointing Angled Coins

Objects that are buried at an angle can be more difficult to locate when you are pinpointing. The ability to find these objects when they are at an angle is more difficult because of how the object is responding.

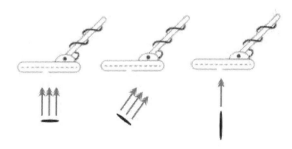

The way to think about this is if the coin or object is parallel to the search head, then the reflective signal it comes back to your metal detector will be relatively accurate. Yet a coin that is at an angle reflects a much narrower signal, as well as the signal, will be at an angle which makes it harder to pinpoint.

It takes time and skill to master the coin or ring that is sitting at an angle to the surface of the ground. After you dig a few really nice coins because nobody else thought the target was worth digging. Your skills will shine compared to your fellow detectorist.

Cleaning your finds

Stop! Your first question should be, should I clean or should I leave the coin alone. It boils down to the value of the coin, is the coin more valuable left untreated? If you are unsure, leave them alone until you can check. Remember the nickel worth $41k, would you try to clean that coin in the field and make it drop to half its value... $20,000, not me.

Most coins made after 1965 are considered modern, clad coins. Their value is a few that have value.

```
2004 WISCONSIN STATE QUARTER WITH EXTRA LEAF - $1499
2005 "IN GOD WE RUST" KANSAS STATE QUARTER - $100
1982 NO MINT MARK ROOSEVELT DIME - $300
1997 DOUBLE-EAR LINCOLN PENNY - $250
1999-P CONNECTICUT BROADSTRUCK QUARTER - $25
2005 SPEARED BISON JEFFERSON NICKEL - $1265
2007 "GODLESS" PRESIDENTIAL DOLLAR COIN - $228
1992 "CLOSE AM" PENNY - $24,000 (Yep $24k that's amazing)
```

What do I mean by clad coins? You can think of clad coins is similar to an Oreo cookie, it is thin layers of different types of metal sandwiched together and then normally plated with a shiny combination of material to make it look pretty. Their value is the value that is stamped on the coin, a penny is worth a penny and a dime is worth a dime.

Most of US coins such as dimes, quarters, half dollars, and dollar coins have a solid copper core, with outside layers of brass or nickel. Except for pennies which today are made out of zinc with a small layer of copper for the surface. The value of the metal within zinc pennies are actually less value of the coin itself.

Many of your fellow metal detectorists will throw these coins into a cleaning solution or possibly a rock tumbler to make them look good. I personally just take them to the store and spend them as is... they are cash.

1965 coins and older

Should I clean, or should I not clean? If you're anything like me I do not memorize all the key dates of every single coin that may have value. My general rule of thumb is if it looks old I leave alone. Even the most innocent act rubbing dirt off the coin to check the date can devalue a good coin instantly.

Let's take a look at an example; you're out in the park hunting for clad coins and you run across the dime that is caked hard with dirt, and the patina is so dark you can't even see the date. Use your thumb to rub the dirt off of dime and find its 1916D Mercury dime. Even the extremely worn-out dimes have a huge value.

1916D Mercury Dime

The act of rubbing and scratching this particular dime could devalue it by hundreds of dollars. In this case, the cleaning of the dime to check the date would've been a huge mistake. This may have been a good candidate for a professional coin cleaner, and they would give you the highest value for your coin.

Your last words of thought before we dive into how to clean coins would be, if you're not sure, leave them as they are.

Cleaning

Clad coins: Probably the simplest and easiest way is to spend a few of those coins and purchase an inexpensive rock tumbler from one of the discount tool stores. I've seen them as cheap as $50 for a single barrel rotary style rock tumbler.

You just dump your coins into the barrel add a few aggregate (which could be aquarium gravel) and a couple of drops dish soap. Turn the machine on and walk away; this will give you a nice shiny coin that you can feel good about spending.

There is also a vibrating style tumbler that works very well, and you can also purchase resin-based abrasives and other polishing mediums from your local rock shop, or metal detecting shop.

Least expensive way to clean these coins is with a toothbrush and a cup of soapy water, plus a bit of elbow grease. You can scrub to your heart's content. Last but not least is the "Coin Star" venting style machine in your grocery store that will accept your coins for a percentage of how much you put into the machine.

Clad Coins (Solutions and fluids)

Run cold water over your coins; this method running cold water over your coin is as safe as it can get without damaging the finish on your coin. You basically can use running tap water, but not under pressure, such as using a sprayer. All you're trying to do is remove the dirt and not damage the surface of the coin.

Soak your coins in warm soapy water - add a couple of drops of mild liquid dish washing soap, into a small container, then drop the coins into this solution and let them soak, this should loosen the dirt and help clean the coin. Avoid using any type of bowl that might scratch the coin, plastic bowls work best. Once the coin has soaked for a reasonable amount of time, put them under the cold running water and see if that helped any at all.

Using small toothpicks, Q-Tips, very soft toothbrush - these tools working getting the sticky gooey stuff off of your coins, but do not use them in excess, you're trying not to scratch the surface of the coin.

White vinegar - white vinegar is an acidic product and it will help dissolve many of the stubborn stains and mild corrosion. You can leave your coins in this solution for a short time, a few minutes up to about 30 minutes. Once you remove the coins from this solution, be sure to run them under warm water

Pat the coins dry, don't rub them dry, the idea is not to create a situation where any extra dirt it on the coin creates a situation where it turns into sandpaper.

Clad Coins (Rock tumblers)

For coins that are only worth their face value or what we call clad coins, a rock tumbler works extremely well. It's just a matter of dropping your coins into the rock tumbler, adding aquarium fish gravel, a small amount of dishwashing soap and letting the machine do the work for you. Your local rock hounds shop, as well as many treasure hunting stores, will have rock tumblers at a reasonable price. The rock shops have different compounds that you can add into your rock tumbler to create the same results as fish gravel, but if you're looking for an economical solution, the fish gravel is very reasonable.

Remember that using rock tumbler is very aggressive and is meant for coins with simple face value. The cost for a rock tumbler starts at about $50 and goes up to over $250. In most rock tumblers will do up to approximately 1 pound of coins and gravel combined.

When in doubt, don't tumble! Take your find to a reputable coin dealer to learn its value before you make any attempt to clean it. These dealers can spot a cleaned coin and will often deem them less valuable just for that reason.

Coins & Jewelry (Ultrasonic cleaning)

Ultrasonic cleaning is a process that uses ultrasound (usually from 20 to 400 kHz) with an appropriate cleaning solvent (sometimes all that is needed is ordinary tap water) to clean items. The ultrasound can be used with just water, but the use of a solvent appropriate for the item can be used to clean and enhances the finish. Cleaning normally lasts between 90 seconds and 600 seconds, but can also exceed 10 minutes, depending on the object to be cleaned.

A relatively good ultrasonic cleaner runs approximately $40. There are a few cheaper in many much more expensive but for the $40 price range you get a relatively decent ultrasonic cleaner.

Rock tumbler

Types of metal and objects

When using a metal detector there are three basic categories of metal that the handheld hobby style metal detectors can detect. There are three basic categories: Ferrous (magnetic), Non-Ferrous (non-magnetic), and Metal Alloys.

Ferrous Metal (magnetic)

Ferrous Metal: Ferrous metals are those metals that are primarily composed of iron and have magnetic properties in them. The common ferrous metals include alloy steel, carbon steel, cast iron, and wrought iron.

Ferrous metals are the most common; the easiest way to determine if it is a ferrous metal is to touch it with a magnet. If the magnet sticks to it, it's considered a ferrous piece of metal. The most common is iron a few examples are: Examples include paper clips, thumbtacks, pins, staples, most screws, nails, washers, welding slag, and rust.

Railroad Spike is an example of Ferrous Metal

Ferrous metals are highly vulnerable to rusting and corrosion when exposed to moisture or an acidic or corrosive environment. Most ferrous metals have good magnetic properties and are considered being good conductors of electricity.

Keep in mind that there are exceptions to all the rules. Wrought iron is one of the exceptions; it is considered a ferrous material due to the nature of this product, yet resists rust.

Non-Ferrous Metal (non-magnetic)

Non-ferrous metals do not contain iron, non-ferrous metals have a higher resistance to rust and corrosion, and they are also non-magnetic.

Non-ferrous metals include aluminum, brass, copper, nickel, tin, lead, and zinc, as well as precious metals like gold and silver.

Examples:
1. Aluminium.
2. Copper.
3. Zinc.
4. Tin.
5. Lead.
6. Silver.
7. Gold.
8. Magnesium.

Metal Alloys

You may think of an alloy as a mixture of metals. To be considered an alloy it must have a minimum of two substances within the mixture, one which is metal. The second component does not necessarily need to be metal and in some cases such as in cast-iron, main metal is iron and it is mixed with carbon to create cast-iron.

Most gold that you find is not 24 karat gold it can be a combination of gold and other metals; such as silver, copper and other substances. Stainless steel is difficult at best detect, the reasoning for this is it is a very poor electrical conductor. Metal detectors need the conductivity of the metal to reflect a signal back to the search coil. Stainless steel is a very low magnetic metal.

Gold rings that you may find are almost always an alloy, which could be a combination of gold and silver or many other metals. Coins can be an alloy and many of the newer coins are considered clad. An example of a clad coin is the newer pennies. They are made up of zinc with copper plating, to make them look like they are solid copper. Within the metal detecting hobby, when these particular coins are buried in moist ground, they will break down really fast and become worthless. Another example is the presidential one dollar coins; they are a combination of manganese and brass.

The older coins (before 1965); an example of this is the silver times; they were an alloy of 90% silver and 10% copper.

Examples of Alloys

Name of Alloy	Metals present	Uses
brass	copper and zinc	Door handles and fittings
bronze	copper and tin	statues
solder	tin and lead	Soldering metals together
stainless steel	Iron, chromium and nickel	Cutlery, kitchen sinks

Iron

Iron is one of the most common items that you'll find with your metal detector. The reason for this is, this metal has been around since the 1700s and people of usage for every conceivable thing that could be thought up. Obvious uses for iron are tools, weapons, construction items, even jewelry.

Over time they've added alloys to iron, in this process they've created steel which is most of the newer items you will find. Most of the time, we consider the small pieces of scrap iron and steel, to be trash items. But these items of trash are really clues to where people have been, and where these trash items are there are normally more valuable items.

Iron, Positive or Negative?

Cast iron, nails, bolts, barbed wire, strapping, tin cans, and are just a few of the items that can register within the iron range on your metal detector. Instead of looking at iron as a negative thing, we should be looking at iron as a clue to where people have been. An example of this would be hunting in the middle of the woods, there is not a single indication anyone ever set foot in the area. Not a single visual indication that a soul has been there in a hundred years. Then your metal detector is starting to ring every time you run across to an iron nail until you get to a point where it seems like the whole ground is covered nails. This is a clue that maybe there was a building there at some point in time. We start to get a clue that people have been there. Why? People lose things… this could be buttons getting torn off clothing or nails from a building or other structure. Maybe these clues are pocket change or loss of the ring while working with farm animals. Next time you run across an area that seems to be littered with a lot of iron, this may be the opportunity to find quality lost items of the past.

Here are a few thoughts on locations where metal parts, junk iron, fence lines, farm equipment being repaired, old automobiles, storage areas, foundations, old outhouses, areas where they may wash clothes or clean, animal pens, trash dumps and living structures that have long passed.

Iron is the most common and by far the easiest for your metal detector to find. Iron seems to leach out which creates a bigger area or gives a halo effect near the object. This halo effect is why nails are easier to detect than a large coin at the same depth.

Iron False Signal

An interesting phenomenon happens when your out metal detecting and you find a target that seems to be large and you dig and dig and nothing is there. I've heard quite a few different explanations for these phenomena, terms such as ghost items, halo effect, iron shadow. In the all of these boil down to what happens to the iron as it interacts with moisture. The iron rusts away, and as it does, it spreads over a larger surface of the ground both towards the surface and away from the surface as well as widening or making the item look much larger than it actually is. Even to the point where the iron item may have completely disappeared, and all is left is a larger shadow that your metal detector can see.

If the item has completely rusted away, you may get a strong signal before digging, and after you dig the item seems to disappear. What's happening is your spreading the iron or rust over a larger area which your metal detector can no longer see this is a normal thing and there is nothing wrong with your metal detector.

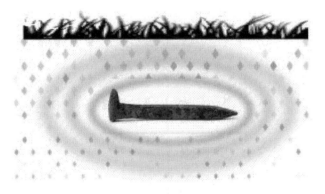

Halo effect

Coin shooting

Most beginners start out hunting for coins in the local parks and school grounds, this is in an effort to teach themselves how to use their metal detector, it's a great way to start hunting. This finding of coins with your metal detector is what we call coin shooting. It is extremely common and many people use this as a stepping stone into other areas of the metal detecting hobby. Many will continue coin hunting and refine their skills to a point where they are looking for very old coins and avoiding the new modern coins of today.

The hard-core veterans consider coin shooting a style of metal detecting where you ignore everything that the metal detector sees except for coins only. This could easily work for you as well as against you, by eliminating everything except coins you could be passing up gold rings, gold necklaces, and bracelets, as well as many more items that are far more valuable than a coin.

Coin Shooting

Most new metal detector hobbyists start out with the dream of finding that first gold coin or a large gold nugget. But the reality is, until you have learned your machine and found many of the newer clad coins of today, it will still be a dream. Finding these clad coins will train you and educate you so that finding a gold nugget is possible within the near future.

You won't get rich finding modern-day coins. But always keep in mind; you never know what you'll find, or how many of these smaller targets you will find in one location. I was out hunting one day, in the most unusual spot, and my metal detector hit one coin, I dug it up then checked my hole. By the time I was done digging that one spot I had dug 19 coins. I wish I could say that they were valuable, but most of the more common coins being a little over the face value. But just having the experience of finding that small bunch of coins in one spot was truly exhilarating.

Coin shooting is not about getting rich, it is about going places enjoying the outdoors and having a lot of fun digging up lost or hidden treasures that have been left behind, sometimes these treasures are newer and have been in the ground for a short period of time, sometimes the item has been lost for years.

Location, Location, Location

You've heard the term "location, location, location." This is true when it comes to finding any type of treasure including coins. When hunting for coins, location is important, you want to go to a place where there have been a lot of people. This location doesn't necessarily have to be a lot of people at one time. If the spot was visited many times over the years and a bunch of people seems to go to that same location, you have much better odds of finding coins, rings, and other treasures. The main idea is going places where a person had a reason to reach into their pocket and pull out money, keys or a reason to search their pockets. These places will give you a much better chance at finding new as well as old coins.

I personally find that the best locations are places like:

- Fairgrounds and rodeo arena
- Churches, Synagogues, Schools
- River beds, Fishing Holes, Swimming Areas
- Beaches, Volleyball Courts

- Playgrounds, Gym Sets, and Kids Play Areas
- Parks, Camping Grounds
- Old towns and stores that have closed

New detectorist tends to stick with the more common locations. These places will have new types of coins and lost items. Take the time to leave your comfort zone and wade into a new location, find something different and enjoy the search.

Meteorite Hunting

General Information

Meteorites are pieces of an asteroid and other celestial matter that falls to the earth. They are those small remnants of shooting stars that actually survive when they fall through our atmosphere meteorites can actually be distinguished from Earth rocks because they are magnetized by their composition of iron, nickel or both.

Hunting for meteorites can be both interesting and potentially valuable. They are far and few between but when you find one of these shooting stars, you have found an item that is rarely seen by your fellow metal detectors.

There are known areas throughout the country that have a higher density of the celestial objects. These zones are considered "strewn fields" the highest yielding states that have these strewn feels as of today is Arizona, Texas, and California. Do not be discouraged, meteorites can be found in every state.

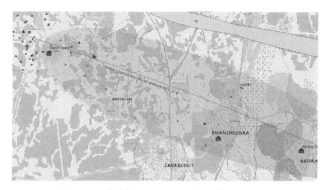

Strewn field is seen in the above picture.

Strewn field is when a larger meteorite breaks up in fragments in the atmosphere and then spreads over a large area of ground. It's normally an oval-shaped area that the disbursement has been made from the midair explosion. The orientation of this oval is usually determined by the flight path where the meteor was coming from. The size of the meteorites tend to be larger at one end of the oval and it the other.

Where to Search For Meteorites

It might seem pretty obvious, but the easiest way to find a meteorite is to go where they have been found before. Normally when one meteorite is found there are many more in the same area, this area could be a very large area. When we say large-area, it could be miles wide many miles long.

One of the best-known meteorite showers within the US borders was the Holbrook in northern Arizona. On the evening of July 19, 1912 thousands of stony meteorites rained down outside a small remote town. This particular meteor shower had thousands about the size of a pea and hearing these small meteorites hitting a tin roof; one eyewitness said it sounded like hailstones. They are still finding these meteorites today.

The best hunting locations include most dry areas with little or no vegetation. The reason for this is that nearly all meteorites contain iron, and iron decays with moisture. The chances of surviving a long time will increase in the drier climates.

Getting Permission

As with anything of value seems the government needs to stick their nose into the casual finding of meteorites. The laws are changing constantly, and these laws are trying to discourage meteorite hunters, your basic warning is; be sure to read up on the BLM laws about meteorite hunting.

The bottom line is that no one has any right to collect meteorites on federal lands for profit or for science without permission of the BLM in the form of a permit.

Can meteorites be collected free of charge and without a permit?

Yes, meteorites may be casually collected, i.e., for free and without a permit, under FLPMA. However, in accordance with the BLM's regulations at 43 CFR 8365.1-5 (1) collection is limited to certain public lands,

(2) only specimens up to ten pounds may be collected per person per year, and (3) only surface collection with the use of non-motorized and non-mechanical equipment is allowed; metal detectors are okay. However, specimens that are casually collected are for personal use only, and may not be bartered or sold for commercial purposes.

Can meteorites be casually collected from other Federal lands, such as the National Forests or the National Parks?

No. This policy only applies to public lands administered by the BLM under its agency authorities. Casual collecting is not allowed on lands administered and controlled by the National Park Service, Bureau of Reclamation, and the U.S. Fish and Wildlife Service.

As with any government regulation there are pages and pages of redundant rules and regulations. But what it boils down to is you can collect meteorites on private property, Bureau of Land Management (BLM), and very few other places.

Meteorite Classification

Stone Meteorite

Stony Iron Meteorite

Pallasite Meteorite

Iron Meteorite

Oriented Meteorite

Positive identification of a meteorite can be difficult and may require an expert. While many meteorites are magnetic, not all are, and a few terrestrial rocks and certain 'rock-like' materials that are also magnetic. The best way to confirm the meteoritic nature of a possible meteorite is to send a small piece (about the size of a fingernail) to one of many meteorite experts, many of whom are members of the Meteoritical Society, including members at universities and museums. These analyses are usually provided free of charge. In the United States and most countries of the western world individuals can own and trade meteorites, original ownership usually going either to the finder or to the owner of the fall site. Many countries, however, claim ownership of all meteorites found in their boundaries as national treasures.

Distinguish a Meteorite from Other Rocks

There many types of meteorites and not all of them are easy to identify. The easiest to identify is nickel-iron meteorites, as they are magnetic very dense and heavy for their size. Meteorites possess characteristics that set them apart. You will need to know what you're looking for when using a metal detector. They will usually have all or most of these characteristics.

Fusion crust: *(a dark, glassy crust produced by melting of its surface.)*

Magnetic: *the meteorites we can find with a detector are* *magnetic.*

Density of the meteorite: *feels heavier than a rock of similar size.*

Thumbprints: *impressions in the rock.*

Iron nickel metal.

Chondrules: *these are small, rounded particles embedded in the meteorite. Visually, it is clear that they were formed at high temperatures.*

If you find a rock that could be a meteorite, do not discard it, and get it tested for. Keep in mind that a few of these meteorites can be quite valuable, and we would hate to see you throw away an exceedingly good find.

Heavy Metals

Historical Uses and Dangers

In our recent past history of mining, there were no laws to protect the individuals. The use of heavy metals such as mercury and lead was commonly used in the mining industry. They would use Mercury in their mining equipment to collect very small pieces of gold. Once the gold was collected in the bottoms of their mining equipment, they would heat the mercury up so it would vaporize and leave the gold deposits. This vapor is extremely dangerous and should be avoided at all cost.

If you are metal detecting looking for gold nuggets

and you run across the lump of silvery heavy metal, the odds are it is an amalgamation of mercury in gold from years past. It is best to just leave the material alone then to risk getting mercury poisoning.

The liquid form of mercury is especially dangerous because it vaporizes at room temperature. When it vaporizes, it fills the air with tiny, invisible mercury atoms that are both scentless and soluble in oils or fats.

Mercury (Hg)

Mercury looks pretty, in its shiny, fast-moving liquid form, **but don't touch!** It can be really poisonous to humans. Mercury is a chemical element with symbol Hg and atomic number 80. It is commonly known as Quicksilver and was formerly named Hydrargyrum. A heavy, silvery D-Block element, mercury is the only metallic element that is liquid at room temperature.

Mercury can form alloys with gold, silver, zinc, and cadmium, which are called amalgams. Through those amalgams, mercury can be used to extract gold from rocks. When mercury comes into contact with gold, the gold dissolves into the mercury and then the two are separated, with the mercury being distilled off.

Why is this important while metal detecting? When metal detecting in gold-bearing areas this chemical was once used to help extract small portions of gold from gold bearing soil. While it was very useful back in the 1890s, we've come to find that it is a dangerous substance. Since this was used so widely back then if you come across to a lump of silvery heavy metal the odds of it being mercury or mercury amalgam is very good. The use of rubber gloves in this particular case is really a good idea. Never handle Mercury with bare hands or let it touch your skin and if you're unsure leave that lie.

Mercury poisoning can result from exposure to water-soluble forms of mercury (such as mercuric chloride or methylmercury), by inhalation of mercury vapor, or by ingesting any form of mercury.

Lead (Pb)

Lead is a chemical element with symbol Pb and atomic number 82. It is a heavy metal that is denser than most common materials. Lead is soft, malleable, and has a relatively low melting point. When freshly cut, lead is bluish-white; it tarnishes to a dull gray color when exposed to air. Lead has the highest atomic number of any stable element and concludes three major decay chains of heavier elements.

Lead is also a poison to most humans and animals, let it lie, and avoid the substance.

Code of Ethics

When we talk about a "Code of Ethics" within the field of our hobby, metal detecting, we are trying to elevate our perception that the general public has about the hobby we have an interest. Preservation into the future is the main goal. The general public thinks of us being hole-diggers, and all we are doing is tearing up their public property, trying to get rich off of the land they love.

This sounds a bit harsh! That is why our code of ethics is so important. If you are anything like I am, I pick up trash and soda cans that have no value, I carry it all day and dispose of it properly. Just like most metal detectorist we will stop, pick up and carry out debris, we all do our best to leave the outdoors cleaner than when we got there.

There will always be a few detectorist that disregard the rules. Just remember that the vast majority of us live by this code of ethics. Don't be afraid to show the hikers that protests, your bag of trash you are removing from their hiking trail, park or beach area. Show them the nails they will not step on, the bottle caps with glass shards that lie just beneath the surface. Educate the public, take a few moments to elevate our hobby.

Metal Detecting Code of Ethics

No leaving of holes and trash you dug up behind.
Protect our woods, forests, and wildlife.
Always ask permission to hunt private land,
and get it in writing if possible.
If you are asked to leave a place, just say,
"Okay, sorry." and leave.
Use thoughtfulness, consideration, and courtesy at all times.
Avoid confrontation with the authorities at all costs.
Don't steal your friend's spots.
Abide by all state and local laws, don't detect cemeteries.
Don't spook, taunt, provoke or otherwise disturb
wild or domestic animals.
Remove and dispose of any trash you find.
No littering of any kind, clean up after yourself.
Leave no trace. Pack out any and all trash or debris you create.
Use common sense and consideration
for others when detecting.
Be responsible, have fun.

All metal detectorist are being judged by the example they set. Always conduct yourself with courtesy and consideration for others. Any hole that is left open will be seen for years. That single hole that was forgotten will put a poor light on our hobby for many years to come.

You'll find that each club, internet site and friends all have slightly different wording within in their code of ethics, but it all boils down to you being responsible for the actions you take while metal detecting.

Why Read Your Owner's Manual?

Your owner's manual has a wealth of information, and of all the reading you should do once you own your metal detector, this is probably the most important part.

It will go through all the basics of how to operate your machine, ways to use it, places you can and cannot take it. An example of this would be many metal detectors are not to be used in water while others have a maximum depth of 10 feet deep of water. This information is within the text of your owner's manual.

Most owners' manual will give you an in-depth look at the functions, parts of the detector, adjustments of your metal detector, and all the features within that particular unit.

This is one of those times where a high-quality machine compared to a low-end machine will have major differences within the owner's manual. Most of the lower end machines give you the basic ideas on how the equipment works, whereas the more expensive machines will have in-depth and highly detailed manuals, which will step you through all the features, advantages and technical specifications of having a good machine.

An example of this would be an inexpensive metal detector may have a manual that has six or eight pages of information where a good metal detector could have up to 75 pages of information.

Laws

State, federal, and local governments have passed many laws. Many these laws affect us directly and impacted the hobby. The main thoughts behind these laws are to protect the historical and archaeological sites on public lands. Many times in your area it will affect private property as well as local, state, federal lands and most waterways. Lawmakers are not trying to disrupt the hobby, but it can be frustrating to us. The laws often affect excavation and removal of objects, which is what most of our hobby is all about.

Spend the time to keep yourself out of trouble, get the correct permissions from the start and avoid in legal issues that might evolve from your lack of diligence. Be sure you find out any rules regarding digging, respect and obey any restrictions for that area.

Private Property - The best way to think of detecting on someone else's private property is to think; how would I like to have someone treat me and my property. We must get the proper permission and it would be best if we obtain written permission, anytime we hunt on private property.

Property owners deserve the respect and care of their property as if it was yours. We need to be professional and continue to be ethical and responsible individuals of the land. Be sure you spend a few minutes explaining your purpose, methods, and techniques to minimize any and all recovery methods. The few minutes spent here will save you hours of finding a new place if you do a bad job or lose confidence with the property owner.

Unfilled holes are unsightly, dangerous to people and livestock, and are detrimental to the continued use of the property.

One more thought on private property, the laws on metal detecting are pretty much straightforward and you can generally dig as long as you have permission, but there are exceptions to every rule. If that private property land has been designated a Native American burial site, an important historical or archaeological site the rules are pretty clear you cannot use a metal detector or dig in those types of sites, no exceptions.

Federal Laws - The intent of this law is: *National Historic Preservation Act (NHPA, 1966 as amended in 2000 and in 2014) directs federal agencies to take into account the effect of any undertaking (a federally funded or assisted project) on historic properties. "Historic property" is any district, building, structure, site, or object that is eligible for listing in the National Register of Historic Places because the property is significant at the national, state, or local level in American history, architecture, archeology, engineering,* *or culture. Typically, a historic property must be at least 50 years old and retain integrity.*

City Property - There is absolutely no uniformity when it comes to the government which includes cities, county, state, and federal government. Even within the city limits, you may encounter places where it's okay to hunt in one park, and then you go into a neighborhood they say no. Don't count on signs to give you an okay or not, a few places will have signs that directly say no metal detecting while others do not. About the only way that you'll know for sure is going to City Hall and asking, and if the city clerk doesn't have a clue, you may end up spending time sitting in her office waiting for her to search through the rules and regulations.

Schools - These places used be considered public, but to be on the safe side permission is always necessary. These spots are normally left up to the school officials to give you permission or not. In this particular case definitely get a permission slip signed.

Beaches - These places used to be considered public, but to be on the safe side permission is always necessary. In this particular case definitely get a permission slip signed.

State or Federal Parks - Detecting at a state or federal park is the riskiest move you can make if you don't have permission. You are practically begging to be arrested if you just decide to start digging without asking.

When you're on federal grounds, in my opinion, you shouldn't even bring your metal detecting equipment with you. Detecting on federal ground carries the stiffest penalties around so you should avoid even the appearance of detecting there.

Archeology Laws

Time Crime: *Protecting the Past in the United States*

An article by Robert Hick (Crime Prevention and Law Enforcement Services, Commonwealth of Virginia) from the Newsletter of the Illicit Antiquities Research Center Issue 9, Autumn 2001

*Laws pertaining to private lands distinguish between surface collecting (picking up objects lying on top of the ground) and any ground-disturbing, or digging for artifacts. Laws pertaining to "State and Federal" lands **do not distinguish** between surface collecting and any type of digging for artifacts.*

A metal detector user may be in violation of the law if artifacts are recovered during metal detecting, or if archaeological sites are disturbed during metal detecting activities. Artifacts and archaeological sites on federal, state, and local jurisdiction-controlled properties are protected by law. Archaeological resources on private property are also safeguarded by law (e.g., trespassing).

Violation of these laws carries serious consequences including the possibility of fines, jail time, and confiscation of the metal detector and other equipment used in the violation (such as vehicles). Other laws may apply including theft, destruction of private or government property, vandalism, and driving in prohibited areas.

Private property - *It is legal to collect artifacts from the surface of private property,* ***IF you have written permission from the landowner****. Be sure not to trespass though.*

On private land, it is legal to dig or metal detect for artifacts IF you have written permission from the landowner, and IF you have notified the Georgia Department of Natural Resources in writing five (5) business days before you begin. This includes all ground-disturbing activities, including on Civil War sites.

It is generally illegal to dig human burials and/or collect human skeletal remains or burial objects. Additionally, it is unlawful to receive, retain, dispose of, or possess any human body part (including bones), knowing it to have been removed from a grave unlawfully.

State property - *To surface collect, metal detect, or to legally dig on any state property, you must have a permit from the Georgia Department of Natural Resources. State property includes state parks, historic sites, wildlife management areas, and state forests, as well as state highway rights-of way, navigable river and stream bottoms, and the Atlantic coast all the way to the three-mile limit.*

Federal property - *Generally, it is illegal to surface collect, metal detect, or dig on any federal lands without a federal permit. Federal lands in Georgia include Corps of Engineers lakes and the surrounding lands managed by the Corps, U.S. Forests, National Park, National Wildlife Refuges, and military bases.*

Care & Maintenance

Most metal detectors are built to withstand your basic use, but they do have integrated circuit boards within the unit. Dropping it or banging it could create damage to the screen, the interior, the plastic housing which keeps the detector water resistant. Handle your metal detector with care. Don't use it as a crutch to help you stand up when you're on your knees digging. It should not be used to push dirt into the hole once you've done your search.

Extreme temperatures also can harm your metal detector. You should not store your metal detector in your hot trunk on a hot summer day. If you live in very cold climates would be best not to store your metal detector in subfreezing weather.

Never use harsh chemicals for cleaning, or solvents are strong detergents. A soft damp cloth will normally do a great job of keeping your metal detector clean. Do your best to prevent any type of water or moisture getting within the control box.

What you're trying to achieve is the longevity of your machine by not causing premature wear and tear of your expenses machine.

The basic of Care & Maintenance
* *Avoid extreme temperatures as much as possible, such as storing the detector in an automobile trunk during the summer or outdoors in sub-freezing*

weather.

• Keep the detector clean. Wipe the control housing with a damp cloth when necessary.

• Disassemble the stem and wipe it and the search coil clean with a damp cloth.

• When storing for longer than one month, remove the batteries from the detector.

• It is best to use quality alkaline batteries. When changing batteries, be sure to replace with all new batteries for optimum performance.

• Replace protective cover on the connector when not using headphones.

Cautions

Here are a few thoughts about cautions you might think about before, during and after your metal detecting hunting.

Trespassing - if you're not sure you're trespassing or not, it would be best if you did not hunt that site. The least that may happen is getting your hands slapped and told to get off the property. But on the worst side, they can confiscate your equipment, give you a fine or worst, which may include your taking your metal detector and anything else related to your hobby.

Underground utilities - avoid these areas which may include electricity, gas lines, telephone lines, and cable.

National Parks, State Parks, Monuments - there are strict rules when it comes to these types of areas within your state. You must familiarize yourself with the rules and regulations, there are no excuses and you can be fined, they can confiscate your equipment, and in extreme cases take your automobile.

Military Zones - this includes active military bases as well as all the battlefields. The biggest danger is unexploded ordinances, bombs, bullets and other dangerous items that could cause harm to you. Most military bases will not allow anyone to metal detect anywhere within their borders.

Uncertain ground conditions - this could mean a multitude of places, from his simple as the edge of a steep bank, areas where sinkholes are plentiful, old mine shafts and caves. These are just a few of the places that you must be careful in or avoid completely.

Trouble Shooting Guide

In most cases, it has been our experience that many of the faults that occur with metal detectors are simple, an oversight or possibly a misunderstanding. The biggest is normally a lack of knowledge, for no simpler reason than skipping the part about reading your owner's manual.

To troubleshooting your metal detector is to read the owner's manual, take a little time, do a little bench testing. The odds are it's a lack of knowledge in the particular area that you're having problems with, such as a misunderstood function setting or something installed incorrectly.

Step one - turn the machine completely off, remove the batteries and let sit for three minutes. This is like when you have a problem with your computer and you don't know what to do, so you turn everything off and let it reset itself. Many times just by turning the machine off will correct many small issues that may be creating your problem. Once the three minutes is over go ahead and put the batteries back in and turn it back on and check to see if the problem still there.

Step two - check for loose connections, broken

wires or dirt and corrosion. Also, keep an eye out for excessive moisture within these connections. Sometimes this moisture will cause a short, static noise or even crackles and grunts when you swing your detector.

No power - if you have rechargeable batteries make sure that they are charged fully. If you have standard batteries make sure that they are installed correctly and if they are old or weak, it would be worth the time spent to replace them with new batteries.

Noise, Chatter and False signals - Check the sensitivity levels, and lower them to see if this is out of adjustment. One of the more common causes of noisy detectors is electrical interference. This could be from nearby metal detectors, overhead wires, in-ground electrical wires, wire fences and using a metal detector indoors.

Intermittent signals - This type of signal the normally found when you have an very deep object. This can also happen when your item is positioned at an odd angle, near other dissimilar items or your discrimination set to "not to see" these objects. Multiple targets and halo effect will also cause intermittent signals.

Moisture - Moisture is bad news when it comes to the electrical circuit. The first thing that you should do is remove the batteries, so this will cause damage through short circuiting the components within your control box. Once the batteries are removed, you should let this dry in a very warm place, and with any luck, after a few days, your metal detector will survive the water. Saltwater is a whole different can of worms. Saltwater is corrosive and is very disastrous to the circuitry within your metal detector and it must be dealt with immediately. It is recommended that you contact your service representative as soon as possible

Understanding the Lingo and Slang

(Lingo or Slang) *"Hey, thought I had a Tatonka, but after I cut the plug I must have had a crap signal with a halo, it was a zincoln, next to a beaver tail and to beat all I dug to China for that."*

What the heck did I just say? Well... I thought I had a Buffalo nickel, but after cutting a hole in the grass, it ended up being a bad signal. It ended up being a zinc Lincoln penny and a pull tab from an old beer can next to each other. Plus it took way longer to find it as if I was digging a hole to China.

Terms and Definitions

Air Test or Bench Testing - Air testing is the process of using your detector to test many type of metal to determine signals, tones at different depths. This is done on a bench or table with the measuring device, such as a plastic ruler to "test" your detectors depth. This is done with several or many objects such as coins or rings tin cans nails to see how your detector works.

All Metal Mode - operating mode or control setting which allows total acceptance of any type of metal targets

Audio VID - See Tone ID (ID = Identification).

Audio Response - see Target Response.

Auto Tune - It is intended to continuously tune the detector's threshold or correct inaccuracies, allowing target rejection or drift to be perfectly tuned despite originally being slightly out of tune from mineralized soil, changes in distance and moisture in the ground.

Barber - the Barber dime (named for its designer, Charles E. Barber, who was Chief Engraver of the U.S. Mint from 1879 to 1917. The design was shared with quarter and half dollar of the same period.)

Bark bandits (Lingo or Slang) - annoying playground kids.

Battery Types - *(Listed are the more common types)*

- *__Carbon-Zinc__ - The most common standard dry cell battery type.*

- *__Nickel Cadmium (NiCd)__ - Is a type of rechargeable battery. A NiCd battery has a terminal voltage during discharge of around 1.2 volts which decreases little until nearly the end of discharge.*

- *__Nickel-Metal Hydride (NiMH)__ - Is a type of rechargeable battery. A NiMH battery can have two to three times the capacity of an equivalent size NiCd.*

- *__Lithium Polymer (LiPo)__ - Is a type of rechargeable battery. They are one of the most popular types of rechargeable batteries for portable electronics, with a high energy density, tiny memory effect and low self-discharge and are far superior to NiMH & NiCd's.*

Note on Batteries - *There is a large number of battery formats and chemical compositions. But the above listed items are the most used with and the metal detecting industry.*

Beach hunters (Lingo or Slang) - Detectorist who mainly hunt beaches.

Absolute Easiest, **Metal Detecting** Guidebook

Beep... beep (Lingo or Slang) - The sound certain detectors make.

Bench Test or Air Testing - An air test to determine at what approximate discriminate settings various metal samples are rejected or accepted. The test is conducted in a non-metallic area.

BFO - Beat Frequency Oscillation, an older detector which uses the induction balance principle. Often used in very inexpensive metal detectors and rarely used in coin shooting anymore. This type of detector is often associated with "old school" detectorist who doesn't want to give up their machine.

Black Dirt – this is organically rich dirt common in very old sites, especially in the Eastern US.

Black Sand - Contain magnetite, it is a black, opaque, magnetic mineral and is one of the most abundant metal oxides. In large enough quantities will affect your detectors signal and adjustment and tuning will be required. These can also be iron particles that are so small they look like sand.

Blanket line – this is considered the first 10 feet of dry sand, from the high tide line.

Bling - Fancy jewelry, which may or may not be precious metal.

Body Mount or Hip Mount - Is basically the main electronic components of your detector that is hip mounted or mounted close to your body to relieve the extra weight of some detectors while swinging it over long periods of time.

Bottle Cap Magnet - A machine that indicates bottle caps as a good signal such as coins.

Bust coin or draped bust - A very old US coin minted from the late 1700s through early 1800s.

Cartwheel (Lingo or Slang) - Silver dollar.

Cache - A hidden store of provisions, weapons, treasure, valuables, it can also mean a large amount of coins or jewelry buried together in a container.

Cache-Hunting - Specifically searching for old caches - requires a different approach to a site than regular coin shooting, since caches were buried in places where specific criteria were met - Such as near animals that would make noise or discourage looters or near landmarks that could be easily found.

Cans Slaw - Shreds of aluminum cans left after being hit by a lawnmower. These give a wide variety of signals due to their size variation and can make for a difficult hunting environment.

Cellar hole / cellar - The remains of a very old home site which had a basement or storage cellar - Sometimes lined with stones, sometimes just a depression. Objects have often been found behind stones or between them. Most detecting finds for cellar holes are in surrounding ground, not in the actual cellar. Hunting near a cellar hole requires great care due to instability of the ground and poorly marked wells.

Chatter - The sound a detector makes when it's running with high sensitivity for maximum depth - A sort of static. You'll often see more advanced detectorist running with a lot of "chatter" to find deeper targets.

Choppy signal - The sound a detector makes when it finds an object that is almost discriminated out. Often used to describe a questionable signal (see also - iffy signal)

Clad - Any of US coin that is "sandwiched" with alloys of different metals.

Coil – (see Search Coil) it's the round thing at the end of your detector.

Coin shooter – is a metal detectorist who looks mainly for coins.

Coin spills - A more generic form of pocket spill - Wherever coins were lost in groups.

Coin Depth Indicator - A visual indicator used in conjunction with calibrated circuitry to indicate depth of buried coins in inches or millimeters.

Cold Stone - This is the opposite hot rock (see hot rock below).

Concentric - A search coil configuration using one or more transmit and one receive windings having unequal diameters aligned on a common center; most recently arranged on the same plane and called coplanar concentric.

Conductive Salts - One of the major mineral types which make up the positive ground matrix. Wet, ocean-salt sand produces a positive rise or metallic type response on an air tuned threshold.

Conductivity - The measure of a metal target's ability to allow eddy current generation on its surface.

Control Housing - A metal or plastic box which holds circuit boards, indicators, meter, controls and power supply.

Convertible/Combination - A metal detector configuration allowing versatility in operator handling, i.e., hand held to body mount.

Coplanar - Any search coil configuration in which transmit and receive windings occupy the same level or plane.

Crystal Controlled Oscillator - A transmit oscillator employing a crystal to maintain stable output frequency.

Depth Penetration - The greatest measureable distance that the detector can transmit an electromagnetic field into the soil and receive signal.

Detection Pattern - The densest or strongest region of the search coils electromagnetic field where detection occurs. Its shape is balloon and changes in size directly proportional to target surface area.

Detuning - Adjusting the audio threshold into the null or less sensitivity tuning zone. Also a method of narrowing a target signal width manually for precise pinpointing. This is accomplished by retuning to audio threshold over the target response area.

Digger - The tool used to dig your targets.

Dig it (Lingo or Slang) - Just dig it up.

Dirt fishing - Metal detecting on soil - Not beaches.

Disc. - Ability of your detector to reject unwanted metal (Also See Discrimination.)

Discrimination - Adjustable circuitry which ignores or nulls audio responses from a specific conductivity range allowing positive responses to be heard from metals higher in conductivity above the discriminate control setting. See also Motion Discriminator.

Display - The target identification on your detector.

Double Blip - A signal characteristic common to elongated ferrous targets such as nails or coins lying close to the surface detected in the All Metal no-motion mode.

Drift - A loss of threshold tuning stability caused by temperature change, battery condition, ground mineral content or detector design.

Dry sand - The sand people lay there blankets and lawn chairs.

Eddy Currents - Small circulating currents produced on the surface of metal by the transmitted electromagnetic field. These currents then produce a secondary electromagnetic field which is then detected by the search coil receiver windings resulting in inductive imbalance between the windings.

Electromagnetic Field - An invisible force extending from top and bottom of the search coil created by the flow of alternating oscillator frequency current around the transmit winding. See also Detection Pattern.

Electronic Pinpointing – this is a feature that automates detuning feature which narrows signal response for the purpose of target pinpointing.

Elliptical Coil - A search coil with an ellipse shape. This coil can be either concentric or wide scan type.

EMI - Electromagnetic interference associated with MDing.

Faint Signal - A sound characteristic of targets that are sometimes deeply buried or very small in size.

False Signal - An erroneous signal created by over shoot, ground voids or highly mineralized hot rocks. See also Back-Reading.

Faraday-Shield - A metal foil wrapping of the search coil windings or metallic paint on search coil housing interior for the purpose of eliminating electrostatic interference caused by wet vegetation.

Ferrous - Descriptive term of any iron or iron bearing material.

Fill or Fill Dirt - Dirt that's been brought in, effectively increasing the depth of old objects/coins. Not a good thing for coin hunting.

Find (Lingo or Slang) - Something you found.

Finds (Lingo or Slang) - The good stuff you found.

Frequency - The number of complete alternating current cycles produced by the transmit oscillator per second.

VLF Very Low Frequency = 3 to 30 kHz;

LF Low Frequency = 30 to 300 kHz;

MF Medium Frequency = 300 to 3000 kHz;

HF High Frequency = 3 to 30 MHz's

Frequency Shift - A feature which suppresses the audio interference (cross-talk) between two detectors using identical transmit frequencies in close proximity.

Gawker - Someone who is intent on watching you metal detect.

Gridding the beach (Lingo or Slang) - Detecting using a pattern as you walk along, most

Ground Balance - an operating mode or circuitry to ignore the masking effect that iron ground minerals have over metal targets.

Ground Balance - Factory Preset - A feature which eliminates the manual ground balance control and its adjustment from the operator's setup procedure. This adjustment is performed internally by the factory to optimize operation over an average range of non-conductive soils.

Ground Balance - Manual Adjusted - A feature requiring a manual control adjustment procedure to neutralize the effects of negative minerals in the search matrix.

Ground Balance - Self Adjusting - A feature which senses change in ground mineral content and continuously readjusts the ground balance while in operation.

Ground Filter – This is a complex circuitry found in motion-type detectors which separates mineral signal from the metal signal allowing it to be further processed by the discrimination circuitry.

Hand Held - A metal detector configuration whereby the operator holds a shaft or handle which supports the search coil and control housing. Also called pole mount.

Hard wired - A modification or quick fix to your detector

Hz, Hertz - See Frequency.

High tone - A beep made by multi-tone detectors when a high conductive target such as silver is found.

Hip Mount - Mounting the control box of your detector with a belt on your waist. (Also see Body Mount.)

Hot Rock - Any rock containing a higher concentration of conductive mineral, which your detector thinks is metallic and give a positive response. **Hunting** - Grabbing your detector and going!

Hunted out / Beat to death - A metal detecting site that has been heavily metal detected over time.

Injun (Lingo or Slang) -Indian head cent.

Indian Head - A US Indian head cent (1859-1909).

Isolator - A nonmetal stem which attaches the search coil to the control shaft eliminating metallic interference in the detection pattern. On some detectors, the entire lower shaft is made of a nonmetal substance.

Keepers (Lingo or Slang) - The targets that you keep whether good or bad

kHz or Kilohertz - 1000 cycles per second. See also Frequency.

LCD or Liquid Crystal Display - Used on a metal detector as a graphic visual indicator same as a meter/needle indicator.

Leave it right (Lingo or Slang) - A very large buried junk target, as in leave it right there.

LED (Light Emitting Diode) - A semiconductor which produces an illuminated visual response.

Loop - See Search Coil.

Loner (Lingo or Slang) - A detectorist that doesn't belong to a club

Matrix - Refers to the total volume of ground penetrated by the transmitted electromagnetic field, which may contain varying amounts and combinations of minerals, metals, salts and moisture.

Masked / Masking - When a piece of iron is nearby a desirable target and alters the way the detector responds.

MDing (Lingo or Slang) - Metal detecting.

MD – this is short for Metal Detector or Metal Detecting.

Memorials - A US one cent piece with the Lincoln memorial on the back (1959 to present).

Merc (Lingo or Slang) - Mercury dime.

Metal - Metallic substances such as iron, foil, nickel, aluminum, gold, brass, lead, copper, silver, etc.

Metal Detectorist – This is the person operating a metal detector.

Meter - A detector component that provides visual information to aid in targets identification. Meters feature either an LCD or needle indicator which may display intensity of signal, target depth, target identification, type of metal, or battery condition.

Mineral-Free Discriminator - Any metal detector that can reject or ignore trash metals while simultaneously balancing ground mineralization.

Mineralized Ground – Is any type soil that contains conductive or non-conductive components.

Mint mark - A special mark placed on coins to let you know where or who made it.

Mode - A condition of operation, selected by the operator, for specific desired function(s).

Morgan – This is a Morgan Silver Dollar. (1878-1921)

Motion Discriminator - A detector type that requires search coil motion to activate its simultaneous ground balance and discriminate functions. See also Mineral-Free Discriminator and

VLF/TR.

Mung (Lingo or Slang) - That nasty seaweed that tangles in your coil while water detecting.

Narrow Response - A target that produces an audio response so short that pinpointing is almost not needed.

Negative Ground - Soil that contains non-conductive minerals which have a negative or nulling effect on an air-tuned threshold.

Neutral Ground - Soil that has no non-conductive or conductive mineral properties.

Newbie (Lingo or Slang) - Someone new at the hobby.

Ni-Cad or Nickel-Cadmium – These are types of battery.

Nice haul (Lingo or Slang) - A comment on your great finds.

Non-Ferrous - Metals of the precious class including gold, silver, copper, etc.

No-Motion - Refers to any mode of operation that does not require search coil motion to trigger target response.

Notch Accept - Operation whereby all target responses are "tuned-out" except those the instrument is adjusted to accept in the notch "window."

Notch Discrimination - Filtering circuitry which allows a "window" of desirable targets to be accepted within the entire rejection range of unaccepted targets, i.e., rejecting nails, foil and pull tabs while accepting nickels and gold rings of the same conductivity. This circuitry can also be adjusted to reject all metal targets while accepting only a specific conductivity range.

Notch Level - A control used to select the target level or target conductivity which the notch filter will act upon.

Notch Reject - Operation whereby all targets within the notch width at chosen notch level will be "tuned-out."

Nugget Shooter – A detectorist that is looks mainly for gold nuggets.

Null - The zone just below audible threshold in metal detector tuning. This also refers to the momentary drop or quiet response of threshold sound as the search coil passes over a discriminated or rejected target.

on-edge — A coin that is buried in the ground oriented up and down, rather than flat (parallel) to the ground surface.

Overlap - The amount of search coil swing advance not greater than the search coil's physical diameter.

Overload - When there is too much metal under the coil for the machine to be useful.

Overshoot - A common false signal heard as the search coil passes over a rejected target when using a no-motion All Metal mode in conjunction with automatic retuning. Excessive tuning restoration pushes the audio above threshold level creating a positive response at the edges of target detection periphery.

Phase Response - The length of time between eddy current generation sustained on a metal's surface and the resultant secondary electromagnetic field effect on the search coils receive winding. **Pinpointing** - Finding the exact target location with respect to a search coil's designated center.

Plug - A hole carefully dug in the ground so that dirt and grass are not harmed.

Pocket spill / coin spill - A bunch of coins lost from ones' pocket or purse.

Positive Ground - Soil which contains conductive minerals or moist salts which have a positive or upward effect on an air-tuned threshold.

PI or Pulse Induction - A mode of operation where the transmitter circuit pulses an electrical current into the ground before it quickly shuts down. The eddy cur rents dissipate immediately from poor conductors such as wet salt sand and ground minerals. Metals hold eddy cur rents because they are better conductors. When the receiver circuit comes on, it picks up the returning signal from metal; the eddy currents in the ground minerals have already disappeared.

Probe - A tool to pinpoint the target while still in ground.

Pull tab magnet - A machine that can't discriminate out pull-tabs very well.

Pulse or PI (Lingo or Slang)l - A waterproof detector that locates all metal targets.

Quick Response - A short time period between metal sensing and peak audio/ visual indicator indication usually associated with all frequency ranges of TR detectors.

Relic hunters - Detectorist who hunts mainly woods.

Rejection - An indication of targets non acceptance by a null in threshold or broken sound while operating in a discriminate mode.

Repeatable - When the metal detecting signal can be repeated in several directions of coil sweeps.

RF-Two Box - A radio frequency detector having its own transmit and receive windings separate and in an orthogonal configuration. This detector is capable of deep large object detection while naturally ignoring small targets such as nails and individual coins.

Rosie (Lingo or Slang) - Silver Roosevelt dime (1946-1964).

Royalty---Sharing your finds with the property owner.

Sand stuff (Lingo or Slang) - Normal trash you find in the sand.

Scan - Refers to 1) - The effective search coil detection width or 2) search coil movement over the ground.

Scrubbing - The search coil is pressed and held in contact with the ground while searching to maintain even audio threshold. With newer detectors, this technique is used to gain depth.

Seeded hunt (Lingo or Slang) – This is a hunt where the finds have been scattered or planted and is a common event in club gatherings.

Search Coil - A circular (or other shaped) plastic housing containing single or multiple transmit and receive windings (wire coils) in a specific configuration. A search coil emits and receives signals from the ground and metal targets, also called loop, coil or head.

Search Coil Cable - An electrostatically shielded cable of conductors (wires) which convey signals to and from the search coil and control housing.

Sensitivity - The capacity of a metal detector to perceive changes in conductivity within the detection pattern. Generally, the more sensitivity a detector can smoothly provide the more depth it will achieve in sensing targets.

Signal - An audio response or visual indication alerting the operator that a target has been detected.

Signal Width - The total distance of ground an audio signal is sustained during search- coil travel or scan.

Silent Search - Refers to detectors capable of producing a target signal while operating below the threshold audio. This can also be called silent operation.

Screamer - A super high quality signal that is loud in the headphones.

Scuff Cover - A protective cover for the search coil bottom. Also called coil cover or skid plate.

Skunked - Hunting and finding nothing of value.

Slow Motion - A description of search coil speed required to operate the motion discriminate mode.

Snippers and snappers (Lingo or Slang) - Small items you find.

Spill (pocket spill) – This tends to be bunch of coins falling out of a pocket.

Stability - The ability of a metal detector to maintain manually adjusted tuning thresh- old under the effects of outside interference. See also Drift.

Surface Area - Refers to the area of a target closest to the search coil where eddy current generation can take place.

Surface Mount - The art of mounting electronic components on the surface of a printed circuit board rather than using the "through board" method. This allows more technology in a much smaller space and with much higher tolerances.

Sweep - The motion employed in moving the search coil across the ground.

Target - Refers to any object that causes an audio or visual response in a detector.

Target VID - A meter or display that shows you what your target might be.

Target Response - See Signal.

Ten-Turn - A control which can be manually rotated ten times to cover the full electrical range of the function. Usually associated with tuning or ground balance function.

Test Garden - A mapped plot of buried targets at various depths to aid in learning characteristic target responses and in comparing metal detector performances under a given ground mineral content. Also called test plot or test bed.

TH'ing (Lingo or Slang) - Treasure hunting.

TH'er (Lingo or Slang) - Universal word contractions for treasure hunter and treasure hunting, also known as Metal Detectorist.

Thingy (Lingo or Slang) - Something you find and don't know what it is.

Threshold - Continuous tone that establishes a reference point for tuning the detector to ground balance it. The threshold tone also establishes the minimum sound level for deep targets in the discriminate mode.

Tone VID - (ID = Identification) Circuitry producing different audio tones for each target's conductivity range, i.e., low tone for nickel, high tone for coins.

Tones machine - A metal detector that requires you to learn the sounds.

Topsoil - First 4 inches of ground.

Absolute Easiest, **Metal Detecting** Guidebook

Tot-Lot-Tour - Areas of parks designated for very young children.

TR or Transmitter-Receiver – This is a term describing method of operation of early detectors. Some manufacturers still produce this type of detector. Electromagnetic field distortion caused by mineralized ground interferes with depth penetration as this type of detector does not ground compensate. It does balance conductive salt water effects so, it is primarily used in salt water and on low mineral salt water beaches or low mineral inland locations.

Tweak it (Lingo or Slang) - Adjusting the detector.

UMO (Lingo or Slang) - Unidentified Metal Object.

VID - Visual ID also Visual Identification.

Virgin site - A location that has not been metal detected.

Visual ID - (ID = Identification) A feature in which a visual indication is produced to help identify the target.

Visual Indicator - A meter, LCD or LED that signals a target's presence.

VLF or Very Low Frequency – One of the types of frequency metal detectors operates within.

VLF/DISC - Term associated with detectors capable of mineral-free operation in both the Discriminate and All Metal modes.

VLF/TR - A class of detector that can operate in both the All Metal, Ground Balance mode and the No-Motion Discriminate, Non-Ground Balance mode.

Walker (Lingo or Slang) - Walking Liberty Half Dollar (1916-1947).

Whatzit (Lingo or Slang) - (see UMO).

Wheatie (Lingo or Slang) - Wheat back cent (1909-1958).

Wide Response - A target that produces an audio signal over an area wider than the search coil diameter.

Zero Discrimination - Used to describe detectors whose discrimination control allows the acceptance of all metals at zero setting.

Zincoln - A zinc-formulated Lincoln Cent, often in poor condition. Not a desirable target.

Easy to Understand,
Metal Detector
Guidebook
How to use guide with
Tips, Tricks and Secrets!

By Steve Cormier
Copyright 2019

Absolute Easiest, Metal Detecting Guidebook

Made in the USA
Columbia, SC
15 September 2020